MW01297126

Table of Contents

Elk Hunting Success is Found Right Here in this Book

In this book, I teach you all of the essentials to achieve the best results possible when getting started in the sport of elk hunting. It is my goal to save you the pain, heartache and lost time that many hunters experience when they first start elk hunting.

Overview:

- The first several sections of this book cover what you need to consider before you hunt such as identifying elk, weapons and how to find where the elk are.
- The second part of this book reveals the "rut", concealment techniques, and using decoys to improve success.
- The final portion of this book covers call types and sounds, shooting techniques, and what to do after you shoot a elk.

Attention All Elk Hunters...

This Is A Step-By-Step Guide To Elk Hunting With No Step Missed!

Easy to Understand Illustrations

In this book, I provide several easy to understand illustrations to help you with the basic concepts of elk hunting. These will help you quickly visualize the concepts explained in the book to be sure you understand each tactic.

Common Mistakes Made by Elk Hunters:

1. Not using the "rut" to their advantage
2. Being "scented" by elk due to wind
3. Incorrect shot placement

How Do You Avoid These Mistakes?

In this book, I will equip you with the knowledge you need to immediately improve your elk hunting success. Put these lessons into action to avoid or discontinue making the common mistakes.

Who Can Benefit from This Book?

I provide relevant information for people with the following experience levels:

- People curious about elk hunting
- People ready to start elk hunting
- Novice elk hunters
- Elk hunters struggling for success

Now let's get started…

Step 1: Why Elk Hunting?

This Huge Animal Makes for Fun Experiences

As we get started, it is important to understand why you would want to hunt elk. There are several reasons to consider hunting elk including its challenges, multiple hunting methods and skills that translate to hunting other game. In this section, I will cover the most common reasons people hunt elk and get you thinking if elk hunting is a sport that is right for you.

Reasons to Hunt Elk:

- Experience new locations
- Relaxing
- Practice for other hunting
- Great exercise
- Challenging
- Taste great & fills the freezer
- Trophy Opportunities

Experience New Locations

Elk hunting is often done in very remote places. Unless you live near prime elk hunting land, you will need to travel to go elk hunting which allows you to experience these new locations. Even if you are hunting in a place that is not all that far away, it will likely be a place that you do not go to on a regular basis. If you are a person interested in elk hunting you are probably interested in the outdoors, so a chance to see some new outdoor terrain will likely appeal to you.

Relaxing

Although elk hunting can require a lot of work, it can also be quite relaxing. This sport forces you to get into the outdoors and experience the wilderness with minimal if any connection to the outside world. With today's face paced and connected lifestyles many people find that elk hunting can help them refocus and relax while they are on their hunting trip.

Great Practice for Other Hunting

One great benefit of elk hunting is that it is an excellent way to learn and teach hunting skills. I am not saying that elk hunting is easy, but it does provide for good learning opportunities. For beginning hunters, the skills you can learn with elk hunting are transferable to other types of hunting, especially big game hunting. The skills include shooting moving game, proper concealment, decoying and stalking. This means that you can use the trial and error that happens during elk hunting other elusive species.

Great Exercise

Elk hunting is a sport that can provide incredible exercise. For example, if you plan on hunting elk with the stalking method, you are going to be in for quite a workout. A single day of stalking elk could include be many miles of walking in an effort to find your game. Often this will include going through some challenging terrain such as tall hills, valleys and thick woods and vegetation. All of these situations will certainly challenge you physically. Before you head out elk hunting, you should put this physical component into consideration. It is best to spend some time in advance getting your fitness up to a level that can withstand these conditions, so you are not left physically exhausted in the middle of your hunt.

Challenging

Once you begin hunting elk, you will realize that this can be a challenging sport but its challenges can make for great enjoyment. To be successful with elk hunting you need to understand elk behavior, concealment, decoying and proper shooting techniques. Unlike some game hunting such as squirrel, dove and waterfowl hunting, the success rates are typically much lower each time you get out hunting. However, this makes the sport fun because it is not a sport that you typically just happen upon having success. So when you are successful, it is satisfying because you were able to fool these elusive animals.

Taste Great

Another reason is that elk can have a great flavor. Unlike some game animals such as squirrels, chipmunks, geese, and even ducks a lot of people find the flavor of elk to be quite tasty. So with elk hunting not only can this be a fun outdoors activity but it can also produce some very tasty and unique meals that you could share with friends and family. It can be a great conversation piece when you prepare elk for visitors.

Trophy Opportunities

If you are looking for a big game trophy that you can be proud to display for years then elk hunting is perfect for you. A bull elk mount is an impressive specimen that you can proudly display for others to admire as they come to your home. Adding a elk mount to your existing game display will undoubtedly turn some heads!

What Elk Hunting is Not

- **CHEAP:** There are all sorts of costs including equipment, travel, license, food, meat processing and taxidermy to name a few.
- **EASY:** Although the sport can be relaxing it is not easy. For successful elk hunting, it will require plenty of physical activity.
- **QUICK:** The most successful elk hunters will invest hours in planning their hunts, studying maps and hours in the field finding elk.
- **WITHOUT RISK:** Sure there are a lot of things you can do to make elk hunting safer. However, there are plenty of risks with the sport including elk charging humans, bear attacks, inclement weather and wilderness survival.

Now let's examine weapon options for elk hunting…

Step 2: Weapons for Elk Hunting

Select from a Variety of Weapons for Hunting Elk

One aspect that keeps elk hunting interesting is the wide range of weapons you can choose from. Each weapon has its own unique strengths and challenges for hunting elk. To mix up your elk hunting, you can try mastering one of these weapons and then move onto another one to experience the satisfaction of filling a elk tag regardless of the weapon you select.

The thing you do want to consider with elk hunting is that they are extremely large animals so you will want to ensure that the weapon you select will have plenty of killing power. This is not a sport for small caliber rifles or low power high gauge shotguns and when you get the chance to take your trophy elk, you don't want to leave anything to chance.

Most common weapons for elk hunting:

- Shotguns
- Rifles
- Bows

Shotguns

Using a shotgun is an effective way to hunt elk that are in close range and even on the run. The reason is that shotguns are often easier to maneuver compared to rifles and bows for quick action. Particularly when elk are on the run the shotgun is going to be your best option as long as they are close enough to hit.

Keep in mind that shotguns typically have an effective range of about 75 - 150 yards with rifled barrels, so you need to plan your shots to be within that distance. There are some extended range choke tubes that you can buy and some ammunition available claims to have further killing ranges but in most cases, you really should plan to be within 100 yards or less of the elk before shooting.

Even with a shotgun, it will be challenging to hit a elk on the run. Not only are they fast, but they quickly change direction when they are running, and the areas where you will find elk can often have many obstructions such as brush or trees in the way. If you are someone who is going to be relying on elk meat as a food source, then a shotgun is a great option. However, if you want to increase the difficulty level of shooting a elk, then you could consider a bow which I will discuss in a minute.

As far as shotguns, there are two different types to select from. There are semi-automatic and pump shotguns. Semi-automatic shotguns automatically load in the next shell after you shoot so you can take successive shots quickly. However, the downside of a semi-automatic shotgun is the cost. These guns usually start around $700.If you are going to be doing other types of hunting such as waterfowl hunting the extra cost to invest in the semi-automatic shotgun might be well worth it. I have had a semi-automatic shotgun for several years and truly enjoy the ease with which you can fire multiple rounds.

The other type of shotgun is a pump shotgun. With this shotgun type, you must use the pump mechanism to load in the next round each time after you shoot. Although there is an increase in time between shots compared to the semi-automatic shotgun, pump shotguns can be very effective, and with some practice you will be able to reload shells quickly. The best part is that pump shotguns are less expensive than semi-automatic shotguns and start around $300 brand new.

Rifles

Another choice you could use for hunting elk is a rifle. There are so many different rifles to choose from it is going to be hard to mention them all but here is a quick list of the various caliber rifles that are commonly used for elk hunting. This is not meant to be an all-inclusive list of rifles you could use, but more a general idea of the great variety of rifles that are commonly used on coyotes.

Rifle Calibers Commonly Used for Elk Hunting:

- 30 - 30 caliber
- 30.06 caliber
- 270 caliber
- 338 caliber
- 300 win mag
- 7mm

Let's discuss the caliber size a little further. Essentially the larger the number of the caliber the larger the bullets are that come out of the gun. For example, a 30.06 caliber bullet is going to be smaller in diameter than a .338. The larger bullets are going to pack a bigger punch when they hit the elk, but the downside is that the larger bullets can do more damage to the meat depending on where you hit the elk. In addition, the larger caliber bullets are typically more expensive than bullets for smaller caliber rifles. Also, the cost of the larger caliber guns is typically the highest. This is not always the case based on the exact brand, features and style, but as a general statement that usually holds true.

So what caliber gun should you buy? Well, I will first say that if you have access to any of these rifle types, you can use them to get into the sport of elk hunting and see what you prefer. I don't think money should get in the way of people having a good time enjoying the outdoors and starting your elk hunting journey. So you can start off by using what you have, or borrow something from a friend or relative. The benefit of borrowing a rifle is that you get to test it out and see what you prefer before you invest in your own.

If you really want the power to drop elk in their tracks, the larger caliber rifles will be an excellent choice. Again you will typically experience a higher cost for the rifle and ammunition for the larger calibers, but if you have decided that elk hunting is something that you enjoy and are willing to invest in a gun that will work for you to bag elk consistently, then go for a larger caliber. Again, smaller caliber rifles can work, but you may find that the power is not always enough to quickly drop elk dead in their tracks. You may end up taking multiple shots to kill the elk or have times where you wound the elk enough to where it dies eventually, but you have to track it for some distance in order to find it.

When hunting elk with a rifle, you will want to do one of two things in order to hit a elk with a single bullet. First, you could wait until the elk is still. The problem is that not often do elk stop moving while you are after them, especially if you have spooked them. However, when they do stop rifles are great for shooting elk. If you do not get a shot at the elk standing still and the elk is now running, then the other way you can be effective in shooting them with a rifle is to be very accurate with your shot placement and pick a specific shooting lane to use. I will discuss shot placement more at a later point in this book, but just be aware that using a rifle will require considerable shooting accuracy when the elk are in motion.

Rifles will come in a variety of reloading styles. One is a bolt-action style meaning that you pull a lever back to load or "cock" the gun after you shoot which brings the next bullet into the chamber. Another style is the semi-automatic style which is where the gun automatically reloads itself after each time it is fired, similar to a semi-automatic shotgun. One more style is a pump style where you use a pumping action on the mid-section of the gun to reload. Typically the semi-automatic rifles are the most expensive where the pump and bolt actions are a little lower in cost.

Accessories to consider for your guns

The most obvious accessory that you will need for your gun is the shells, but there are many other accessories that you should consider for elk hunting such as scopes, slings, extended-capacity magazines, and tripods. These accessories can make your elk hunting experience more enjoyable and productive.

Accessories to consider for rifles:

- Scopes
- Slings
- Extended-Capacity Magazines
- Tripods

Scopes

If you plan on hunting elk with a rifle, you may want to consider investing in a scope. A scope is similar to binoculars where it helps magnify distances, making far-away objects appear closer. Having a scope is excellent for shooting at elk that are sitting still and at a long distance. In this case, a scope will allow you to place a very accurate shot on your elk. However, one of the downsides to a scope is they can make moving targets harder to shoot. This is because they magnify all of the surroundings which can make it disorienting and difficult to find your target that is on the move.

Think of it like trying to watch something through binoculars. When the object is still, binoculars are great to see the item close up. However, if the object is moving it can be hard to locate it and keep track of where the object is. The other downside can be their cost. Entry level scopes start around $50 or so, but if you are looking for a scope that has further distance abilities and other features you could easily be looking at several hundred dollars.

Slings

You will often have long walks when stalking elk so a sling can be a great way to make carrying your gun easier. Basically, a sling is a strap that attaches to both ends of your gun and goes over your shoulder to free up your hands. This allows you to carry other items and makes it easier to go over some of the difficult terrains you might encounter outdoors.

Slings are usually inexpensive ranging from about $10-$30, and you can purchase them from any sporting goods store. To use a sling, your gun will need to have sling mounts. Basically these are round metal knobs that have holes through them where you can attach your sling. Slings will have a fastening system that slides easily through these holes. If you have a gun that does not have sling mounts, you can go to a gunsmith, and they can add them to your gun for about $30.

Extended-Capacity Magazines

Some guns have the option to add an extended-capacity magazine. Basically, these serve the purpose of allowing you to hold more bullets in the magazine than what is possible with the standard magazine that the gun comes with. These are primarily used for rifles and are not generally offered for shotguns but can be found with some searching.

The standard capacity of a magazine for most rifles is usually around 5-6 bullets. However, with an extended-capacity magazine, they could hold anywhere from 10 to 20 rounds or even more. When you are taking several shots at elk, these extended-capacity magazines can be very convenient. These are particularly useful if you have a semi-automatic rifle as you can make many shots in just a few seconds.

Tripods/Bipods

When you are hunting with rifles, it is important to be able to hold your gun steady for an accurate shot at elk. One way to accomplish this is to buy a tripod or bipod for your rifle. Basically these is made up of two small plastic arms that attach to the bottom of your rifle allowing you to place the rifle on the ground and use these arms to steady the gun in position as you shoot. Tripods work well for steadying your gun if you plan on shooting from a lying down position. For those of you who want to shoot from a sitting or standing position, a rifle stake will be useful.

Bows

For hunters who are looking for an additional level of challenge to elk hunting, you could consider hunting with a bow. Bow hunting has been around for ages and used for taking a variety of game animals. As of recently, bows have become even more popular for elk hunting. Part of this increase in popularity for the use of bows in elk hunting is the increase of people using bows for other hunting big game, so now that more people already have a bow it is exciting to use it for other hunting.

Your range for shooting elk with a bow is going to be significantly less than a shotgun or rifle. For the highest probability shots with a bow, you should plan on being within about 15-40 yards of the elk. Due to how close you have to be in order to shoot a elk with a bow it can really make for an exciting but challenging experience.

A few other challenges to mention about using a bow is the learning curve. Learning to use a bow and learning to shoot at distances accurately will typically take someone much longer than it would with a shotgun or rifle. People often practice months or even years before they get to be average at efficiently shooting with a bow. In contrast, most people could learn to shoot a gun well enough to hit a still animal with just a few days of practice.

However, after pointing out the downsides of bow hunting, I do not want you to be discouraged with the thought of using them for elk hunting. As I have already mentioned, it can be a thrilling experience to hunt with bows because you are going to be much closer to the elk for shooting and that can be exciting. In addition, many people like bow hunting because of the personal satisfaction that they get from using this more challenging way of hunting versus a shotgun. Shotguns and rifles are great weapons, but you really do have a significant advantage over the game you hunt with them because of some of the killing distances you can achieve. Using a bow level the playing field with elk and thus increasing personal satisfaction when you successfully bag a elk.

Now let's identify essentials to bring on your hunt...

Step 3: Field Essentials

Bring these Items to Prepare for Hunting Elk

Now that we have discussed weapon types and shells let's take a look at some of the other items that you may want to bring with you on your hunting trip. I am going to cover the major items in this section, but there may be other items you want to bring after you hunt some and realize what you prefer to have within the field. These items should give you a good start on what to have with for a fun and successful elk hunting trip.

What else should I bring with hunting?

- Clothing
- Face Paint/Face Mask
- Hunting blind
- Chair
- Bear Spray
- Shooting stick
- Hunting knife
- Bone saw
- Binoculars
- Rangefinder
- Bug spray
- Toilet paper
- Compass& GPS
- Food & water

Clothing

One primary key to hunting elk is remaining well concealed from their sight. You will need a camouflage shirt, pants, hat, and gloves. When it comes to hunting clothing, I do recommend buying the best quality that your budget will allow. Long days of hunting can become challenging and not much fun if you are not warm and comfortable. Plus a higher investment up front in hunting clothing will typically result in clothing that will last you for years of hunting. You should look for fleece or wool clothing for elk hunting as they no not much, if any noise when walking.

In addition to camo clothing you may need to have blaze orange clothing as well. Some areas will require at least the top ½ of your body to be covered in blaze orange to allow other hunters to see you. This is most common during firearm seasons as the distance that firearms can reach is quite long. With bow hunting, you can often wear just camouflage. A good option if you are required to wear blaze orange in your area is to get a blaze orange vest. This way you can put the vest on over your camouflage jacket. This saves you from having to buy a camo jacket and orange jacket. For example, I use the camo jacket for duck hunting then can use an orange vest over the camo for big game.

To keep your feet warm and dry you will need to get a nice pair of hunting boots. Again, this is an item for hunting that you will likely want to invest a little more in to ensure good quality. Try and find high gram count boots as the higher gram Thinsulate they have, the more warmth they will provide. One other tip when buying hunting boots is you typically want to buy them one size larger than the normal size you buy for shoes. This is because you will be wearing thick socks and you want to ensure there is room for these thicker socks as well as a little extra space for the air to be trapped. Boots that are too tight can actually cause your feet to get cold fast.

Face Paint/Face Mask

In addition to camouflage clothing, another method you can use to take concealment to a higher level is utilizing face paint. Depending on how well you are concealed from the elk it is possible that the elk could see the skin on your face and be scared off. A simple solution to this is to buy a few tubes of camo face paint and apply it prior to elk hunting. A tube of face

to push so hard to cut which will reduce the chances of the knife slipping and you cutting yourself.

Bone Saw

A great complement to your hunting knife will be a bone saw. Bone saws can be quite handy because you will most likely need to quarter out your elk to carry it out of the field. Although I will discuss this process in depth later in this book, it is essential to know that it is simply not feasible in most situations to carry your elk out hole. So you will need to cut it into sections so you can take a few trips to get your entire elk back to your camp or home. Using a bone saw for this process will be critical and most hunting knives will not be up to this task.

Binoculars

Investing in a set of binoculars for hunting is an excellent way check out your surroundings. The great thing is you do not need to spend a significant amount of money to get yourself a pair of binoculars to increase your viewing distance. For several years I used a set of binoculars that I purchased for $20. Sure there are more expensive pairs you can buy, but even the cheap binoculars can significantly improve your viewing distance.

One of the most useful times to utilize binoculars for elk hunting is when you are hunting on the side of an open field. With binoculars, you can see to the other side of the field and the edges of the fields on the other side as well as checking treelines. They will help you be able to identify what kind of elk is approaching well in advance of the elk coming within shooting distance. You will also find binoculars useful as you scout for elk. When driving around you are able to look out the window and check for elk in fields, on the ground and look for elkroosting in trees.

Range Finder

In addition to investing in a good pair of binoculars, I would also recommend investing in a rangefinder. It can sometimes be quite challenging to accurately judge distances with the naked eye. Sure there are hunters and guides with years of experience that are quite good estimating ranges without any electronic assistance. However, to newer hunters or hunters who want to be sure, they have the proper range before making a shot a rangefinder is an excellent addition to your hunting equipment. In particular, if you are going to be using a high powered rifle for long distance shots the aming of your shot is determined by the distance the bullet will travel. Bullets will drop elevation after a certain distance so without knowing exact yardage you may end up shooting over or under the elk.

Toilet Paper

Honestly, it is a great idea to bring a roll of toilet paper within your hunting backpack. If you plan on having a several hour elk hunt then there is a chance that you will have to use the restroom at some point. The good news is that the outdoors will provide many areas where you can use the restroom in a concealed spot. Unfortunately, if you do not bring toilet paper and nature calls you may find it necessary to cut your hunt short and head out for a restroom. Do yourself a favor and throw a roll of toilet paper in a ziplock bag and put it in your backpack in case of emergency. Storing the toilet paper inside of a ziplock bag ensures that it will remain dry.

Compass & GPS

Depending on the location you are going to hunt, and how familiar you are with the area you are in, it can be a great idea to bring a compass with you. Any time that you are hunting a new area, you should bring a compass for safety. Especially if you are going to hunt on public land that you have not hunted before it would be a good idea to bring a compass. If you have a compass app on your phone that would work great so you don't have to carry an additional item with you. However, the downside is many compass apps require reception, so if you are in a remote area without reception they will be useless. The other risk is if your phone runs out of batteries you will now be without a compass.

Besides just a compass you should also bring with a portable GPS device. This would be highly recommended particularly when you hunt areas where there is no cell phone service which is many of the remote areas where you will likely be hunting elk. A compass is a great backup if the batteries run out on your GPS, but a GPS can really make life easier. You can see the terrain that you will encounter so you can plan your hunts better. Also, many GPS systems have location markers you can set so you can mark spots you have seen elk as well as your base camp location.

Food & Water

I do recommend bringing some water and food with on your hunting trip. When you are going to hunt for just an hour or so a bottle of water and a snack bar should get you through. Having just this little bit of food and water can help keep you hydrated and energized. When you plan longer trips, you may want to bring a few bottles of water and even pack a lunch. Without food and water, you might have to stop hunting sooner than you want. With some food and water you can extend your hunting trip, particularly on those days when you are having good success.

Now let's find out discuss why using a guide service to get started can be a good idea...

Step 4: Guide Services

What Are the Benefits of a Guide Service?

Anytime that you are doing something new it can be beneficial to learn from someone with expert knowledge. Just think back to when you first started to learn a new skill in school, let's take math for example. Sure you may have been able to look at assignments and read a book in an attempt to try and figure out math on your own. However, it is usually much easier and faster to be taught by someone who has years of experience on the subject that can share their expertise to accelerate your learning.

With elk hunting, this can be a good reason to start out your hunting education with a guide service. A skilled and experienced guide will be able to share their years of experience with you and teach you tactics along the way that will not only be helpful to you to bag a elk while on your guided trip, but that knowledge can also help you prepare for venturing out elk hunting on your own in the future.

What Type Of Guide Services Are Offered?

The good news is that there a wide variety of services offered by guide services based on the type of trip you want to experience, area you will be hunting and your hunting skill level.

Fully Guided

The first type of guide trip to put into consideration is a fully guided elk hunt. Fully guided means that a guide will be with you during the entire trip from the start until you are able to harvest a elk or until your designed time has expired. Fully guided trips are great for the novice hunter as well as hunting in areas in which you have no familiarity with.

Sometimes these fully guided trips also include helpers and cooks preparing meals for you along the way on your trip or back at a basecamp prepared by cooks. If you are looking for a hand holding trip where most of the preparation and work is done for you, then fully guided trips are your answer. However, a downside to the fully guided hunts is the cost. In fact, in some cases, a fully guided elk hunt can cost as much as $25,000.

Unguided

The complete opposite of fully guided trips are fully unguided trips. These trips are typically designed for experienced elk hunters and people with plenty of outdoors experience including survival skills. Of course, this depends on the area you are going on your elk hunt. Especially for those excursions that are into remote areas you want to be sure that you have plenty of outdoor and survival experience before venturing out on your own.

The big benefit of doing a fully unguided elk hunt is the personal satisfaction it can give you. Sure it is exciting to have a guide to work with and get you into a great opportunity to harvest a elk but doing this all on your own can be very rewarding. The other benefit of fully unguided elk hunts is their cost is often significantly lower than fully guided. Unguided hunts may range from 40% - 60% of the cost compared to fully guided.

Unguided with Outfitter Camp

One happy medium from fully guided to fully unguided elk hunts are unguided hunts with an outfitter base camp. These hunts will take some of the prep work off of you because you will have a base camp that is taken care of by the guide service but during the days you are able to venture out on your own to hunt elk. You have the reassurance and peace of mind that you get to return to the base camp each night for a warm place to stay and a good meal.

Additionally, when you are struggling to find a elk, the base camp guides will likely be able to give you some advice on what to do differently in order to have a successful hunt and other areas to try and locate elk. The price for these experiences are typically in the middle of the price range from $2,500 - $10,000. Of course, there are a lot of factors that will impact the pricing with all of the options mentioned above such as length of hunt and the region you are hunting.

Cost Difference (Estimates)

- Guided - $3,000 - $25,000 +
- Fully Unguided - $2,000 - $15,000
- Unguided With Outfitter Camp - $2,500 - $10,000

Where to Find Elk Guides?

In most places with populations of elk that can support hunting, you will also be able to find elk hunting guides. Now finding a guide will depend on a few factors and one of the biggest is going to be the area you want to hunt. Additionally, due to the high cost of going on a guided elk hunt, you want to ensure that you find a trustworthy and experienced guide before sending in a large deposit.

Contact Government Wildlife Offices in The Area

An often overlooked yet highly effective way to find an experienced and trustworthy elk hunting guide is to contact the government wildlife offices in the area you want to hunt and ask for a recommendation. This is because the government wildlife offices will have plenty of experience with all of the guides in their jurisdiction and can tell you which guides are good and which ones to stay away from. In addition, if the government requires guides to be, they can often send you a list of licensed guides to look at so you can make sure that the service you hire has all necessary qualifications to legally provide the service.

Regional Guide Outfitters Associations

Some areas have guide outfitters associations that are a great resource to find hunting guides. These associations have many guide services that are registered with them to show the guides validity, and some also help with conservation efforts. If you a web search for "guide associations" in the area you are hunting you can see if that area has an association. For example, in British Columbia, the association is called the "Guide Outfitters Association of British Columbia" and can be found at www.goabc.org. The site has a search function to help you find guides for the type of hunting trip you want to take.

Ask For Recommendations on Online Forums & Social Media Groups

Another efficient way to find good hunting guides is to search through internet forums and social media groups and ask the members for recommendations. For example, you can go on social media sites and search "elk hunting," and you will find several pages and groups that discuss the sport of elk hunting. You can make a post to the page and ask people for recommendations of guides to use in the area you are planning to hunt.

You will typically get several great recommendations from these groups, and sometimes you will even connect directly with a guide who is a member of that group. However, one word of caution is to do a double check of any guide before booking. One efficient way to do this is to contact the government wildlife office in that area and ask them about that guide service. You will likely get a very honest answer, and they can validate if the guide has all necessary requirements to provide the service.

Use a Hunting Guide Broker

Another good option to find a hunting guide is to use a hunting guide broker. Hunting guide brokers work with a wide range of hunting guides, and their job is to connect people looking to go on guided hunts with hunting guides who provide the services. The great benefit of using a broker is that it will reduce the amount time you need to spend researching hunting guides as well as shopping for prices that fit your hunting budget.

You simply tell the brokers your budget and type of hunt you are looking for, and they will work to find you a matching guide. To find a hunting guide broker, you can simply go online and search for terms like "hunting guide brokers," and you will find several. The one downside of working with a broker is there is usually a fee associated with going through the broker compared to going to the hunting guide directly. However, as I mentioned they save you a lot of time and they can also set you up with trusted guides they have worked with in the past, so you know you are going to have a quality experience.

Now let's find learn about licensing and hunter safety…

Step 5: Licensing, Hunter Safety and Rules

Make Sure You Have the Proper Licenses and Any Applicable Safety Registration

It is important to make sure you have the proper licensing and learn hunting safety prior to heading out for a elk hunt. The laws and regulations for elk hunting are very different from one area to the next. This means that you will want to check all regulations in your planned hunting area to ensure that you are fully compliant with all applicable laws. Additionally, you may need to have some type of safety certification to hunt elk which is in addition to the license you need to harvest a elk.

Legal aspects to consider before hunting:

- Area you are hunting
- Specific hunting dates
- Bulls, cows & calves
- Safety certification
- Hunting rules

Area

When you are going to purchase your hunting license, the first thing you will need to know is what area you plan to hunt. In some areas, elk hunting licenses are good for the entire state that you purchase the license in, but if you will be hunting in multiple states then you will probably need multiple licenses. Be aware that if you are not a resident of the state you plan to hunt in you will typically pay a higher rate for your license. Sometimes it can be as much as double, if not more, then what it costs for a resident of that area to buy a license. However, in some states, there are different zones which are sections of the state that are predetermined by the wildlife office. Certain zones may have different hunting restrictions.

You should also consider what other type of hunting or fishing you plan to do within that year before you buy a hunting license. Some states allow you to purchase a combination license that will give you hunting and fishing privileges for a slightly discounted rate. Not only do you save a little money this way but it also helps reduce the amount of paperwork you need to carry with you.

Hunting Dates

In addition to knowing what areas you plan to hunt elk, you will also need to know the dates you plan to hunt them. For example, the region may have 4 or 5 different seasons for hunting elk. Each season may run only 1 or 2 weeks long, and when you buy a license, it is only good for one of those seasons. Spreading out the licenses by dates helps keep the number of hunters in one area restricted to improve hunter safety during each period. Also, you should consider what is best in your area compared to the elk rut. Typically the earlier dates are before the primary rut; middle dates are during the peak of the rut and late dates after the rut. There are benefits to each part of the rut which I will discuss later.

Bulls, Cows & Calves

As I mentioned earlier, there are bulls, cows and calf elk. When it comes to hunting elk, there are going to be rules on what type of elk you can shoot. In some areas, you will only be allowed to shoot a bull elk. In some areas, you may only be able to shoot a cow elk and some areas may not have any restrictions on what type of elk you shoot even if it is a calf.

Also, sometimes these type of elk restrictions are determined by the time of year. For example, young calves can struggle to make it through a winter without its cow mother. So in some areas shooting a cow in the fall will not be permitted as it could also hurt the changes of her calves surviving as well.

Just be sure you understand the regulations and that you properly identify the elk before you pull the trigger. Unfortunately, not knowing the rules is not a valid excuse if a game warden catches you without proper licensing for the elk you just shot. The penalties can be very harsh for people who violate the rules including loss of hunting privileges, jail time and confiscation of hunting equipment.

Lottery

Another consideration when planning your elk hunt is the lottery process that is required in many areas for elk hunting. What I mean is that it is not often where every single person who wants to hunt elk will be allowed a permit to do so. The amount of elk that are allowed to be harvested in one area on a yearly basis is determined by the wildlife agency to preserve the elk population.

If too many elk are harvested, it could significantly impact that areas elk population going forward. However, if too few elk are harvested it could also cause issues such as a lack of food for all elk to survive as well as impacts to public safety. Too many elk near highly populated areas can increase vehicle accidents with elk.

The point to this is that you must plan well in advance of when you want to go on a elk hunt to ensure that you can have a license for the hunt. In fact, there are some areas that have deadlines for elk permits over a year in advance. If you miss the application deadline, it could put your hunt off at least one year, if not longer, if you are not drawn for a elk tag in subsequent lotteries.

Safety Certification

In addition to having proper licensing, you will also need to ensure that you obtain any necessary safety certifications prior to hunting elk. Again, the rules in each area are different. In some areas, you will need to have a formal safety certification regardless of your age. In other areas, if you are over a certain age, you do not need to have safety training.

Even if your area does not require any safety training, it is an excellent idea to go through a safety training course prior to doing any type of hunting. Although hunting can be a very fun activity, it also comes with a certain level of safety risk.You can never eliminate all safety risks when hunting, but going through a formal safety class will teach you valuable skills to improve your safety practices. Hunting safety courses often range from $20 to $100 for a course that will last a few weeks. The great thing is many areas offer the coursework part of safety certification online. This way you can learn of the book skills needed while in the comfort of your home. Then at the conclusion, you go and take a field day test to prove your firearm knowledge and safety understanding. This is a great investment in your long-term safety.

Other Safety Factors

- Tell someone where you where you are hunting and when you will be back. In case you get lost, hurt or otherwise someone can send for help if you do not return on time.
- Be aware that elk might get angry and charge at you. Look for raised hair on the back and neck of a elk as well as flattened ears. These are all indicators that the elk might be getting ready to charge you.
- Lookout for bears. In many areas where you will find elk, there can also be bears present. Pay attention to signs of bears as well as carry bear spray in case you encounter one while hunting.
- Ensure you are familiar with the area. It is best to not go to an area you do not know. When hunting new areas be sure you study the terrain on maps in advance and carry a map and GPS with on your hunt.
- Bring plenty of water for your trip. Regardless if it is just a few hour trip or a few days ensure you have enough water as elk hunting can be physically exhausting. Ensure to drink enough water, so you do not become dehydrated.

- Understand the physical conditioning needed to hunt elk. Often times elk hunting will be done by traveling long distances in woods and hills to find elk. Take time to prep your body for this in advance. Also, if you do successfully harvest a elk, there will be a lot of work to carry the elk out of the field. Ensure your body can handle this task.

Now let's take a look at useful tools for elk hunting…

Step 6: Identifying Bulls, Cows, and Calves

Learn to Identify Elk Before Hunting

It is extremely important to know how to identify elk quickly and before you shoot so you shoot the correct gender and not make a mistake of shooting the wrong one. Identifying elk will come easier as you hunt more often, but this will give you a brief overview of how to identify elk. The good news is that there are really only three variations of elk to identify you should be able to identify them quickly with just a little bit of practice.

IDENTIFYING ELK

Bull

Cow

Calf

Bulls

The bull elk is most often what you will be going after when you are elk hunting. The bull elk is the adult male elk. Bulls are easily identifiable by the large antlers they have on their head. These wide antlers are called their "rack" and are usually identifiable from quite a distance away making mistaking a bull elk for something else pretty unlikely. In addition, the bull elk are usually much larger than female elk and depending on region can get up to about 700 pounds!

Cows

Female elk are most often called "cows" and are going to be somewhat smaller than the male "bull" elk. Cow elk can range from 400 – 500 pounds depending on region. In addition to the size difference, other identifiable features between the cow and bull is the lack of antlers.

Now even though the cow elk do not have antlers, it does not mean that a lack of antlers means that the elk is for sure a cow. This is because bull elk shed their antlers in the winter and regrow them fully over the next few months. So if the area you are hunting allows spring hunting and you are after a bull elk be sure to identify the target by more than just the presence of antlers. However, most areas do not allow hunting outside of the fall, so antlers are likely going to be your best form of identifying a bull from a cow.

Calves

Lastly, we will discuss the calf elk which can either be male or female. Basically the calf elk is a juvenile elk. Their size will depend on how old the calf is, but they will be noticeably smaller than the bull or cow elk as they range from about 300 – 400 pounds. Now when trophy hunting for bulls you are probably going to pay little worry about shooting a calf elk. However, be aware that there are some areas that do allow hunting of calves to help manage the elk populations. Particularly in the fall because not all calves make it through harsh winters so wildlife departments may intentionally allow calf permits to thin the population. Additionally, harvesting a "spike" bull is often permitted with a bull license. A "spike" bull is a young bull but rather than having a large rack of antlers they will have two antlers that point straight up in the air versus several different tines that face all directions like the full grown bulls.

Now let's learn about elk habitat and food sources…

Step 7: Habitat & Food Sources

What Do Elk Eat and Where do They Live?

When hunting any species, it is useful to know what they eat and where they are found. Armed with knowledge of what elk commonly eat can help you figure out prime hunting locations because if are setup near where elk eat then you are more likely to have success. In this section, I will cover some of the most common types of food that elk eat and where you can often find elk.

Where Elk Are Found?

Elk are found through several of the northern parts of the United States much of Canada as well as Alaska. Some of the specific states in the USA include Montana, Kentucky, North Carolina, Pennsylvania, Michigan, Wisconsin, Missouri, Virginia and West Virginaia to name a few. Other areas around the world include Newfoundland, New Zealand, and Russia.

Where Do Elk Hang Out?

Now that we know that you can find elk in several states in the USA and most providences of Canada let's take a look at where you are likely to find elk hanging out. These are some of ideas on where to start to find the elk, but of course, there are more areas as well. As you hunt more in your area, you will start to see what areas the elk are located at most often.

Near Food

One of the best ways to improve your chances at harvesting a elk is to be near an area where the elk are going to feed. Like any animal, elk need to eat, so it only makes sense to find them near their source of food. You will find that elk in the area you hunt may prefer one food source over another or perhaps you hunt in a region where one food source is more abundant than others. For example, elk enjoy eating leaves, twigs, and branches so if you find an area with plenty of low hanging branches and leaves you can likely expect to find some elk frequenting that area.

What Do Elk Eat?

- Leaves
- Grass
- Twigs
- Branches
- Water Plants
- Tree Shoots
- Willows
- Birch Trees
- Fir Trees
- Lily Pads

Near Water

All animals need to drink water at some point which means that setting up near water is likely in a spot where you will eventually see some elk. Ponds, rivers, lakes, and streams are good areas where it will be common to find elk drinking and feeding on water plants. This makes hunting locations that are in between tree lines and water sources a great place to set up for elk hunting. In particular, during the rut cow and calf elk will often hang out near shorelines during the day. If you are looking to bag a cow or elk this makes shoreline hunting a great option. Also, since bulls will be on the search for a cow to mate with the shoreline will make a great place to intercept those frisky bulls.

Woods

Another favorite spot for elk to hangout is the woods and woods that border fields. Woods can be particularly productive during warm days. This is because the elk will want to get out of the direct sunlight to catch some shade to cool down. When you are making walks through woods for be sure to not only look for elk that are standing up but also check alongside standing trees and trees that have fallen down. Elk love leaning up against these natural backrests as they take a warm day snooze.

Open Areas

In addition to woods, elk also like to hang out in open areas. This includes fields, prairies, and grassy areas just to name a few. As an example, a grassy field is a prime spot to find elk in the mornings and late afternoons. These open areas allows the elk plenty of sight distance to watch out for any potential predators as well as good viewing for bulls to find cows. Find yourself a concealed area on the side of a field, and you could be in for some pretty good elk hunting.

Now let's find out how to use the "rut" to your advantage when hunting elk...

Step 8: THE "RUT"

Enjoy the Opportunities Created by Elk Behavior

When planning your elk hunt, there are going to be several factors to consider when picking your hunting dates. If you have a choice of hunting dates, you will also want to consider how the "rut" will impact your hunting. Let's take a look at the "rut" this interesting part of elk hunting and what each time of the rut provides for hunting excitement.

What is the rut?

First off, let's discuss what the "rut" is in case you are not familiar. The "rut" is the time of year when elk are mating. If you hunt other game animals such as deer you may already be aware of this term since many other game animals are hunted during the rut as well. Basically the male elk will be out searching for female elk who have not yet mated. Additionally, during this time of year, it is not uncommon for the males to fight over being able to mate with unmated females.

Rut Timing Seasons:

- Early Season (Pre Rut)
- Mid Season (Rut)
- Late Season (Post Rut)

Early Season (Pre Rut)

In the early season of elk hunting or the "pre-rut" the elk typically have not yet begun to mate. However, the bulls are going to start to become much more active, and they will start behaving in ways to help them find a female mate. For example, they will often start making rubs and thrashing through grass, saplings and small trees. The bulls make the identifiable rub markings on trees and saplings as a way to identify to cows in the area that they are there and ready to mate. In addition, the bulls use these rubs as markings to signal to other bull elk that this is their territory. Early season elk may be in some higher elevations so be sure to keep an eye out on the ridgelines and hills to see if you can spot a trophy elk!

Mid Season (Rut)

As the season progresses further into the fall, then it will be time for the full rut, often times in the first weeks of October depending on your hunting location. This is the prime mating time for elk and can be an excellent time to go hunting. One of the best things about hunting during the rut is that elk can become somewhat less wary as they focus so much on mating that they may make mistakes that they would have otherwise not made that can allow you to harvest a very nice elk.

For example, a bull elk might not often leave himself out in exposed open areas for long periods of time. However, if he is chasing after a potential mate, he might just chase her out into the open, and this mistake could allow you an opportunity at a clean and unhindered open shot while he focuses on getting his mate. This is what makes hunting during the peak of the rut the best time to hunt elk if you can do it.

Another reason that makes the rut a great time to hunt is that cow and calf elk will often hang out around water. Find those lakes, streams, ponds, and rivers in the area you will be hunting and keep an eye out on those shorelines for these relaxing elk. If you have a cow or calf tag, these shorelines will be prime areas to bag your elk. In addition, the bulls will come by these shorelines as well as they will be searching after the cows. So regardless of what type of elk you are hunting, shorelines during the rut can be a great hunting location.

Late Season (Post-Rut)

Even though the rut will eventually end, it does not mean that there is still not a chance to bag your elk during this post rut time. In fact, the good news is that some elk hunters may give up if they have not yet filled their tag by the end of the rut but if you are willing to stick it out and look for post rut opportunities you can still be in for a great hunt.

The first thing to understand when you are going for post rut elk is that they have lost interest in finding mates, especially if they have already mated. This means that if you are hunting a bull elk that you should not expect that they will respond to cow mating calls. You can also put your cow elk decoys away during this time. In fact, the bulls will often become more isolated from cows during this time, but you may actually find them with other bulls.

Also, during this post-rut hunting time, you will need to understand that the elk are now focused on preparing for the winter. So rather than spending their efforts on tracking down a mating partner, they are now focused on finding quality food that will help them prepare a bulk up for the long winter months. This makes hunting near remaining late season food sources a great place to bag bull elk. Late season elk often push further into the woods so be prepared for a bit more of a challenge as they will not always be standing out in open areas for you to see. Get your legs ready for a good hike to find these late season bulls.

A key to successful elk is timing your hunt, here are some tips...

Step 9: Timing Your Hunt

How Time of Day Impacts Elk Hunting

After you have identified what part of the rut you are going to be elk hunting you should also consider what time of day you plan on hunting. If you have elected to use a guide service, you will likely be hunting all day every day during your designated trip length. Or if you are hunting independently, you might have found a way to clear other responsibilities, so you can spend a few days hunting during all shooting hours. However, if the amount of time you have to hunt during the day is limited, you should consider when you want to spend that time chasing elk.

Time:

- Morning
- Mid-day
- Sunset

Morning

The first few hours of sunlight can be some of the absolute best times to hunt elk. Like many other animals, elk head out for their first meal of the day shortly after sunrise. Likely they have gone the entire evening without eating so now they should be hungry and will head to nearby food sources. This is a great time to be positioned along paths to their feeding grounds. As the elk make way to their food source get ready for action.

In addition, elk will also often drink within the first few hours of daylight and as I mentioned. This means that setting up to hunt with a good view water sources can be a great morning hunting spot. All of these reasons that make elk active in the first few hours of the morning a great reason to hunt elk in the morning.

Mid-Day

After the first peak hunting hours of the morning, the activity of elk typically slows down during the midday. Depending on where you will be hunting the hours will vary, but this could typically be the hours of approximately 11 am to around 4 pm. During the midday the elk tend to be less active and rest during these times. However, I do not want you to get discouraged from heading out for a elk hunt in the midday. Even though the active elk numbers may dip during this time, if you have scouted your location well and have patterned nearby elk you can still have a successful hunt.

To be successful in the midday you want to be where the elk are. Most elk have probably had their first meal of the day by now but may still be looking for something to drink or even searching for a mate. Try finding ridgelines where elk have trails through the woods and set up on a spot that is within shooting distance. As the elk walk along these paths, you should be in good shooting position.

In addition, you can identify locations that elk will be bedding down and resting during this time. During the midday the temperatures typically warm and since elk like to stay cool during these times, they often bed down in shady places. You might find them inside of the forest under thick tree cover, next to willow patches and sometimes in open areas where there is some taller grass or plants that they can use as cover. Particularly when there is some snow on the ground, this is somewhat more common as even though they are in the open the snow will help keep them cool. One more place you can find elk during the warm afternoons is alongside water. They may be resting on the shore of a lake, stream or river to stay cool and an added bonus is they are close to food and water as well.

Sunset

The last few hours of sunlight provide excellent shooting opportunities, similar to the first few hours of the day. The behaviors that elk had in the morning will typically be repeated before it gets dark outside. The elk want to fill up their bellies in preparation their restduring the evening hours. This means that the elk will be back out to feed and may even return to the same feeding spots that they visited during the morning. Additionally, they will likely want to get something to drink before the sun goes down. So check all of those favorite spots you scouted out for your morning hunt and try them again before sunset.

Another key to successful elk hunting is scouting, here are some tips…

Step 10: Scouting for Success

How to Select the Proper Location to hunt elk

As with most hunting the more time you invest finding the spots where your game is located, the higher the chances are that you will be successful when you head out for the actual hunt. This holds true with elk hunting as well. Let's take a look at some ways to improve your elk hunting success with a little preparation in advance.

Identifying Areas for Elk Hunting:

- Study maps in advance
- Pay attention to where you see elk
- Checkless frequented areas
- Prairies and fields
- Woods
- Near water
- Near food sources

- Use trail cameras
- Look for tracks
- Observe for droppings
- Tree scrapes
- Rut pits
- Scent pit
- Wallows
- Bedding areas

Study Maps in Advance

Before you even head out scouting for elk, you will probably have an idea of the region you want to hunt in. At this time take a look at some land maps and look at the terrain. This can save you a ton of time when out driving around and looking for elk because if you narrow down some areas based on what appears to be good elk territory, you can narrow in on those areas right away.

After you determine the area you are going to hunt in you should invest even more time studying topographical maps of that area. You really want to have a good understanding of all of the terrain in advance of your hunt. Google earth in satellite view can be a good starting point, but there are other more advanced maps for topographical views that you can buy online that will be handy in advance and area also helpful to bring with on your actual hunt.

Finally, it is important to have maps to mark where you see sign of elk. Later in this section, I will discuss some of the elk signs to look for. However, the important thing is to be able to track and log where you see elk sign. By having a good record of this, you can try and pattern the elk which this knowledge will come in useful as you head out on your elk hunt.

Pay Attention to Where you See Elk

This should be obvious, but you want to pay attention to where you see elk. When you are driving around keep an eye out in the fields and woods and actively look for elk.If you often see elk in a specific area, this should be a great place for you to start. Also, you can ask your friends and family to be on the lookout for you. Let them know that you want to go elk hunting and ask if they could pay attention to what they are seeing. It is better to have several people searching for elk rather than doing it alone and often time's friends and family will be willing to help you out with this.

Another strategy to get the feedback from others on good places to hunt is to make a posting to your favorite social media website and let people know that you are looking to go elk hunting. Ask and see if your friends have suggestions on where to go. This is a great way to get the word out to a lot of people at once, and oftentimes people will be willing to help you out and provide some ideas. If people do not know that you want to hunt elk, there is no way your friend can help you out. You may be pleasantly surprised on the success you have in finding a spot for elk hunting when you simply ask for help.

Check Less Frequented Areas

Depending on the area you live and plan to hunt there is a chance that there are some areas where a lot of people hunt. There might be one easy to get to wildlife area that makes scouting easy for people because there are side roads and easy access. However, the problem is if you follow what others do and go to these easy to get to spots you will likely be battling with others for this same territory. If you can try and get out into some more of the remote areas that less people go to and even get out of your vehicle and walk around looking for elk sign. Yes, this will be more time consuming up front but this extra time investment might be worth it to find a elk heaven that will be productive during the elk season.

Prairies and Fields

Open prairies and fields can be good places to hunt for elk. These open areas are excellent hunting grounds as the elk can see long distances and be aware of any predators as well as search for easily accessible food. This, in turn, makes for good hunting spots because as the elk are out searching for their food, you can be out searching for the elk.In addition, prairies and fields are good for hunting because you usually have great viewing distances to spot those elk. Try and find the higher spots and tree lines to sit near because they will give you increased viewing distance as elk come out of hiding while keeping you concealed from their sight.

Woods

Although woods are a good place to find elk, woods are also a challenging place to shoot elk. The trees, branches, and leaves can make it challenging to see elk in this type of environment. Once a elk starts running in the woods, you will have minimal time to be able to shoot it. They run very fast and the further away they get from you the more branches and leaves that will be in your shooting lane to the elk.

When hunting in the woods, it is best to try and find an area that has somewhat of a clearing. This will allow you to have a little more of an opportunity to shoot at the elk without much in the way. Areas, where you hunt for elk, are often the same areas where people hunt for deer or other wild game. The great thing about hunting in an area that is used for deer hunting is that there are likely going to be some deer hunting stands that you could use to sit in for hunting elk. Anytime you can get to a high spot you are put at an advantage as you can see longer distances. In addition, by being elevated up in the air, you are put out of the direct line of sight of the elk.

Near Water

For elk, you will often find they rest relatively near a water source. A great place to check for elk is in tree lines that border ponds, rivers, and lakes. Another reason why hunting near water is good is because all animals need to drink water at some point, so it is likely you will eventually see some elk. In the late fall season during very cold days any open water spots can be a prime spot for hunting because as most water has frozen over the few spots that are open and easily accessible are going to be highly frequented by elk.

Use Trail Cameras

A fun way to validate that there are elk in the area you plan to hunt is to utilize trail cameras. Basically a trail camera is a camera that you can attach to a tree, fence post or other stationary item in a high traffic area. Then the camera captures pictures when there is motion anywhere in the area. You can affix the trail camera by wrapping straps around the tree at a height that will pick up the image you are trying to get, for elk this would be about 3-4 feet off the ground.

Trail camera technology has come a long way, and it is truly amazing what you can do with them now. Many trail cameras operate with a memory card system where you plug in a memory card, and any pictures that are taken are stored on the card. You can then view these images on a computer, or even some mobile phones can pull images from the memory card. In the recent years, there have started to be some trail cameras that work with an internet connection, so any images taken by the camera are sent directly to your mobile phone for instant viewing. This is really great because it saves you the time and money of driving to your hunting spot several times to check the memory card. However, the downside is the trail cameras with this feature are significantly more expensive than the standard memory card style.

Look for Tracks

Another sure-fire way to know if there are elk in the area are to look for elk tracks left on the ground. However, you may not always see these unless there is soft ground, mud or snow on the ground. Hunting for elk in the snow or after a recent rainfall when the ground is soft will be some of the best times to be able to see where elk are traveling from the footprints they leave. The prints consist of two long hoofs with almost an elongated teardrop look on each. You will notice that they look similar to other deer tracks as elk are in the deer family but one thing that will help set them apart is the sheer size of the print. Elk prints made by bulls and can get up to 7 inches long and calf tracks will usually be in the 4-inch range.

Observe for Droppings

Another indicator of elk in the area is their droppings. Elk droppings are often described by people to have the resemblance and size of a chocolate covered almond. The elk droppings otherwise called "scat" will be brown in color and about 1 inch long. Color and consistency can be different based on what the elk has been eating.

As you walk through the woods and fields be sure to take time not only to observe the ground for prints but also look for droppings on the ground. If you find a pile of droppings, you should stop to examine them. If the droppings have a wet appearance that means that the droppings are fresh and that the elk was in the area recently. When the droppings have a dried out appearance that means they are older, but it can still be a good sign that elk may still be living nearby.

Tree Scrapes

Using their large antlers bull elk will often create scrapes on several trees in their territory. They simply rub away on the trees with their antler racks in order to create visible indicators to other elk in the area. Be observant of the trees as you are walking and look for rubs that start from about 2 feet to all of the ways up to about 6 or 7 feet off the ground. Fresh rubs will be very bright in color and will have green around the outer ring of the scrape on live trees. As scrapes get older, the will dull in color and look more dark brown, eventually turning nearly the color of the rest of the non-rubbed bark on the tree.

Wallows (Also Called Scent Pits and Rut Pits)

Elk wallows are areas of dirt that bull elk dig out with their hooves. They tend to be fairly large, several feet in length and width making them large enough for the bull elk to lay in. Bull elk will make these wallows during the rut as a way to attract mates. They urinate in the wallows and then will lay and will often cover their antlers in this mud and urine mixture. The hopes of the bull is that this strong smell will attract cow elk. In addition, cow elk that come across these wallows will be able to smell that there was a bull elk in the area. If the cow elk has not mated yet, they might wait around for the bull elk to return. You may actually smell a wallow before you even see it due to their strong smell.

Bedding Areas

Another indicator of elk in the area is their bedding areas. Essentially these are the elk lay down to sleep and rest. These can be in a wide variety of areas including grassy fields, tree lines and deep inside of the forest. They will be large oval areas that where the natural vegetation is compressed. For example, if a elk beds down in a grass field, you will easily be able to see a section where the grass has been flattened. Often times elk will continue to use the same bedding areas for months if not years as long as they are not disturbed. If you can locate bedding areas, these make great spots to set up nearby to harvest elk as they come and go from their resting activities.

Now let's discuss how to find land to hunt...

Step 11: Finding Land to Hunt

Public Land Can Provide Excellent Hunting Opportunities

Similar to private land, with a little effort you can find some great hunting spots available on public land. If you are like me and do not own land to hunt you will either need to get permission to hunt private land, find public land to hunt or hire a guide service.

Types of public lands available for hunting elk:

- Wildlife Management Areas (WMAs)
- State Forests
- Wildlife Refuges
- National Forests
- County Land

Tips about using public land:

- Search online
- Contact your state wildlife office
- Scout out the area in advance
- Be safe

Search Online

With a little online research, you may be able to find some public hunting land within a reasonable driving distance from your home. Simply search online using any of the terms listed above under "Types of public land available for hunting elk" followed by your state or county name and you may be able to be a listing. Each state has different regulations for these areas so if you have questions regarding hunting regulations that are not clearly denoted online, be sure to reach out to your state wildlife office directly.

Contact Your State Wildlife Office

State wildlife officers are usually very friendly people and passionate about the outdoors. Don't be afraid to call the wildlife office and ask them what areas they would suggest nearby for elk hunting. They want to help people enjoy the outdoors so if you ask, they are going to be happy to assist. Additionally, they understand the importance of properly managing the elk population in preservation of a healthy environment, so they will likely be motivated to help you find a place to hunt elk.

Scout the Area in Advance

Once you have a site in mind, if possible, it is great to scout out the area in advance. Try driving to the hunting location a few days prior to hunting and review the territory. Take a walk and note if you see any elk. Even if you are unable to physically go to the hunting spot in advance, you can use online resources to help you plan your hunt. Since you may have found this location by looking online for public hunting areas, you can usually find online maps for these public lands. Scan those maps to determine where you will hunt and the route you will take to your hunting spot in advance.

Safety

Safety is the primary thing to be aware of when hunting on public land. Since it is public land, anyone can use this land, and there is no way to guarantee that you are alone. It is important to check your surroundings before you shoot. You may find it easy to get caught up in the excitement of shooting and forget what is around you. However, you first want to think about what is in the direction you are shooting can be dangerous at quite a distance can travel a long distance. You need to be one hundred percent sure that there is nobody in the vicinity that could possibly get hit. If you are ever in doubt if you have a safe shot, do not shoot. What makes elk hunting even more dangerous is the fact that hunters wear camouflage to stay concealed and they are also likely to be using a elk decoy. This means that someone not paying attention could shoot at a elk decoy and end up hitting a hidden hunter behind it.

Hunting Private Land: Tips for Asking Permission

If you are like me, you do not own hunting land and don't always want to battle other hunters for public land. In addition, many areas prime for elk hunting often private property. At first, it can feel a little uncomfortable to ask other people to use their land for elk hunting. However, after some experience, the process gets much easier. Also, if you get permission to hunt on someone's land one time, they are likely to let you come back again in the future.

Tips to get permission to hunt private land:

- Don't be afraid to ask
- Don't wear hunting clothes when approaching them to ask
- Be kind and smile
- Bring a youth hunter if possible
- Tell them exact times you will be there
- Do a favor in return
- Bring them meat or another gift
- Thank them after

Don't Be Afraid to Ask

Something that holds hunters back from finding land to hunt is the fear of asking for permission. People can feel intimidated by asking landowners for permission to hunt on their property, but the more you do it, the more you get used to it. When you are turned down for permission the primary reason is usually that they already have a friend or family member that hunts the area.

Sample wording to use when asking permission:

- Hello, my name is ___, and I am hoping to do some elk hunting tomorrow. It seems like you have a great piece of land for elk hunting. Would it be okay with you if I hunted on your property this weekend?
- Good afternoon, I am looking for a place to elk hunt with my friend tomorrow. Would it be possible for us to hunt on your land for elk for a few hours in the morning?
- Hello, I was driving by your property on my way to town last night, and I saw a elk in your field. I really enjoy elk hunting, and I'm wondering if it would be okay with you if I could hunt here for a few hours this afternoon.

If they say no, don't waste this opportunity to find a hunting spot. Thank them and ask them if they know of any other places nearby that they would suggest trying. They might know another landowner that would allow you to hunt their property or they might know of some good public land for hunting in the area.

Don't Wear Hunting Clothing

I recommend not wearing hunting clothing when you go to ask for permission to hunt on someone's property because it can give the landowners a feeling that you are assuming that you will be able to hunt there. Not all people like or allow hunting so don't assume anything. If you are planning on hunting that same day, at least take off your camouflage clothing. It should not take too much to remove the items that make you look like a hunter. If you are dressed like you are ready to hunt, it can also give them the impression that you may go hunt on their land even if they do not give you permission.

Be Kind and Smile

This should go without saying, but if you are polite to the landowner, they will more than likely be polite back. Be conscious when you approach the property to put a smile on your face to ensure that you are received as a friendly individual. Do what you can to strike up a conversation with the landowner by asking them some questions such as how long they have lived at the property or what they do for a living. People love to talk about themselves so if you can get the conversation going and let the landowner talk, it will likely improve your chances of getting permission to hunt their land. If they do agree to allow you to hunt on their property, keep the conversation going and ask them where on their property, in particular, they would recommend hunting. After all, they should know best where the elk have been on their property.

Bring a Youth Hunter

Most people have a soft spot for children so if you are planning to hunt with a child it can help to bring them with you when you ask for permission. People who would have said no to you alone may say yes if it means that a child will get the opportunity to experience the outdoors. Another benefit of bringing a child is that it can be a great learning experience for the child. This helps get the child used to speaking to strangers and helps them learn all of the aspects of hunting that will be valuable to them when they start hunting on their own.

Tell Them the Exact Times You Will Be There

To help put the landowners at ease, it is important to let them know exactly when you plan to hunt. If you want to hunt just one morning, tell them that. Or if you want access for an entire weekend, be specific, so they are not taken off guard when they see you on their property. This is very important because people will feel more comfortable knowing the exact times that they can expect to see you rather than having you show up at any random time of the day. Never go hunting on someone else's property at a time when you do not have permission.

Do a Favor In Return

Landowners often have work that needs to be done around their property, particularly if they are farmers. Ask them if there are a few projects that you could help out with for an afternoon or two in exchange for hunting on their property. Not only would assisting with these chores be a way to get permission to hunt, but it is also a great way to form a relationship with the landowner. The more you get to know them, the more likely they are to let you to continue to hunt there.

Bring Them Meat or Other Small Gifts

Another thing you can ask is if the landowners would like to have some meat in exchange for allowing you to hunt there. Even if they don't hunt, most people may like getting some free meat. This can be a great win-win situation for both parties. Compared to other game animals, elk is one of the better tasting wild game, so there is a good chance they would be interested in sharing some of the meat with you.

Additionally, other small gifts could be a way to say thank you to the landowner for allowing you to use their property. You could bake some cookies in advance or stop at the store on the way and buy some cookies to give them. It does not have to be anything very expensive, but something simple can go a long way in letting them know that you appreciate their generosity in allowing you to hunt on their property.

Benefits of Getting Permission Effectively

If you follow these steps and are respectful with those who allow you to hunt their land, you may end up with one or more long-term hunting spots. Be kind when asking, do something in return, and get to know the landowners. The better the connections you make with people, the more likely you will be to build a great network of landowners and have multiple hunting locations that you can use.

The next section includes considerations to keep in mind as soon as you get to your hunting spot…

Step 12: Arriving at your Hunting Spot

Your Chances of Success Start as Soon as You Arrive at Your Hunting Spot

It is extremely important to be aware of every little detail when you arrive at your hunting spot and as you walk to the spot where you plan on hunting. Elk are wary animals; this means they will notice things that are out of the ordinary and will do their best to keep a good distance away from humans.

Pay Attention to Little Details to Have Elk Hunting Success:

- Arrival Path
- Noise
- Timing Your Arrival

Arrival Path

To start off with it a good idea to park a good distance away from your hunting location. Elk are able to see and hear vehicles approaching so be sure that you park your vehicle at least several hundred yards away from the location you plan to hunt. Although it is not always fun to walk a long distance, your hunting success can be greatly compromised when parking near your hunting spot.

As you walk from your vehicle to your hunting location, you should also pay attention to your cover along the way. What I mean is that you should try and stay as concealed as much as possible as you make your way to the hunting pot. For example, you are often going to be hunting along the tree lines of fields or other open areas. These open areas are great because you can see the elk from a good distance away without much obstruction when you want to aim and shoot.

However, these open areas also present the same clear line of sight for elk that may be in the area to see you. So you must keep this in mind to improve your hunting success. Most fields are going to have some type tree line or taller grass or vegetation along the edges of the field. By walking along these the natural cover, you will keep you a little more concealed rather than blatantly walking across an open field. Of course, there is no way to walk to a hunting spot without any chance of being spotted but being aware of movement you are making can help reduce the chances of alerting nearby elk.

WALKING TO YOR HUNTING SPOT

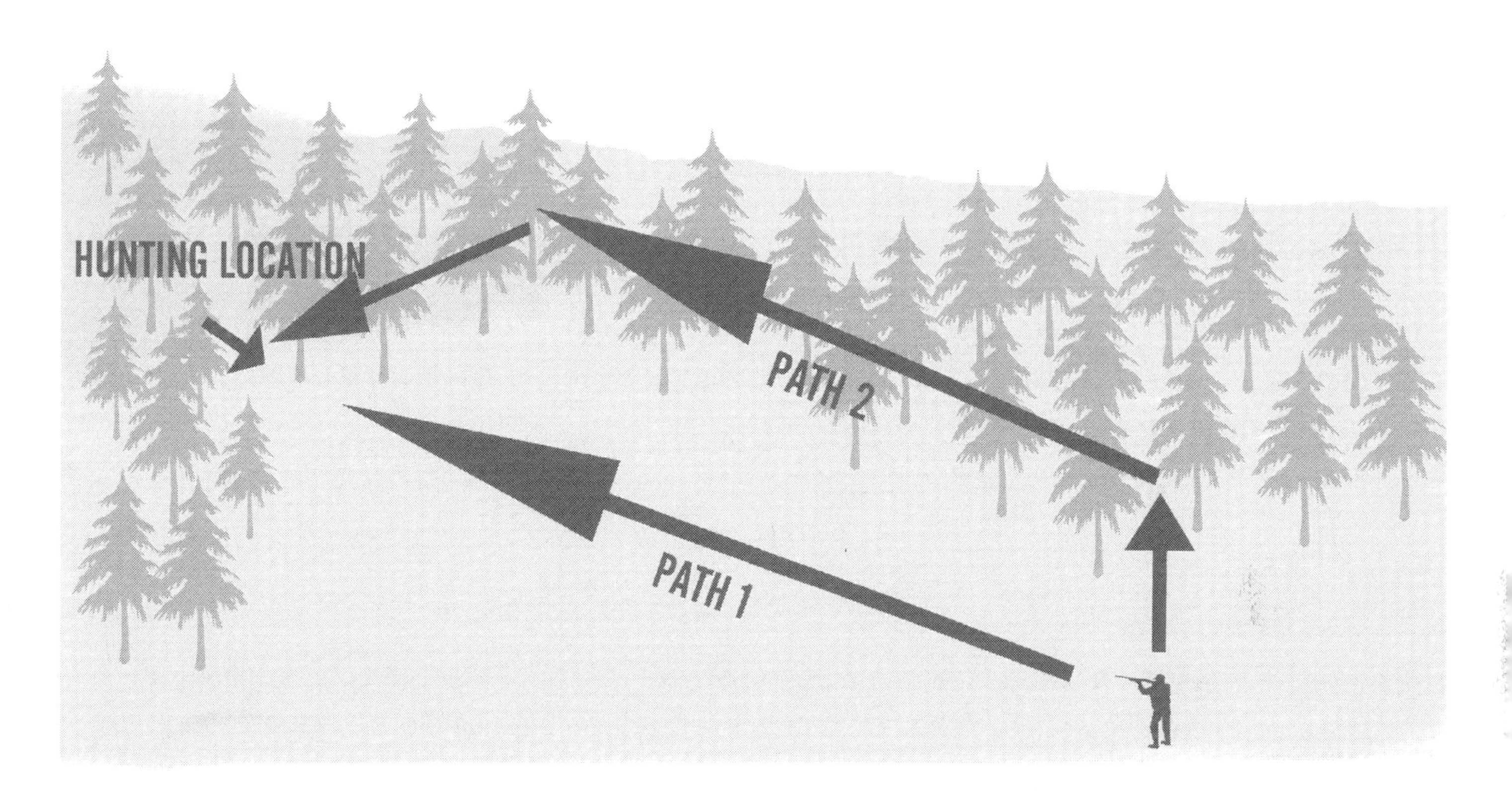

As you can see in the illustration, there are two paths that you could use to walk to the hunting location, path 1 or path 2. In the example, the hunting location is on the left side of the open field surrounded by trees. The hunter plans on hunting from underneath a few trees there as it should give clear shooting lanes and long viewing distances into the field, it is also where he has recently seen elk. Path 1 shows the clearest and most accessible path to get to to the hunting spot. This is because anytime you are trying to get somewhere the shortest way is to go in a straight line. Additionally, since this is an open field, there is not much in your way so he will likely not be stepping over fallen down trees, battling thick brush or have much difficult terrain to navigate.

However, path 1 has a significant downside in getting to the hunting spot, and that is the fact that he will be out in the open for a long period of time while he is walking. This entire time he will be exposed to the sight of any nearby elk and will likely scare them away making the long walk entirely wasted. However, what he can do to reduce the chances of being spotted is by using path 2. As you can see with path two, there is a tree line that the hunter is going to walk within to stay concealed. He is going to walk several yards into the tree line to use the trees as a natural covering to conceal his movement and body. Path 2 is longer in distance, uphill, and likely has more vegetation to get through making for a more challenging walk but ultimately choosing this path over path 1 can be beneficial.

Of course, the illustration is just an example of how you can get to your hunting spot and reduce your chances of being seen. The area you are going to hunt is most likely going to be different, but this section is to help you understand the concept that it is best to stay out of wide open spaces as you walk around for elk hunting. Even though finding paths with more cover are likely to take longer and may be more difficult to navigate, staying out of the sight of elk can help keep from scaring the elk away.

Noise

Another consideration to keep in mind as you arrive to your hunting spot is controlling the amount of you noise you make. Of course, it is pretty much impossible to eliminate all noise but being aware of the noise you are making and doing as much as you can to reduce it will decrease the chances that you scare away elk. Elk do have an excellent hearing, so every little bit you do in reducing noise makes a difference.

Be aware of these noisemakers:

- Shutting vehicle doors
- Talking
- Stepping on sticks/leaves
- Loading weapons
- Setting up decoys
- Setting up hunting blinds

Timing Your Arrival

The final item to discuss when planning our arrival at your hunting spot is the timing. In general, you should plan to be at your hunting spot well in advance of your legal hunting time. For example, the legal shooting hours in your area might be from ½ hour before sunrise to ½ hour after sunset. In this example I would recommend planning to be sitting and fully set up in your hunting spot at least ½ hour before legal shooting time. This means you will need to plan on leaving much earlier than that to account for the time it will take to walk to your hunting spot and getting any decoys or blinds set up. This is because you will want to allow some time for the area to settle back down before elk start getting active. If you are setting up equipment later and the elk start moving there is a good chance you will scare them away before ever seeing them. Being setup ½ hour in advance is a good recommended minimum time to be ready, but some people prefer to allow an hour or more.

Next, we will look at how to use sun to your advantage when elk hunting…

Step 13: Sun Impact

Using The Sun to Your Advantage

One tactic you can implement to improve your elk hunting success is utilizing the sun to help keep yourself concealed from elk. It's important to do anything you can in order to reduce chances of being spotted by elk. This means that the sun can play a key factor in elk hunting success.

First off, the sun can be blinding to you as you try and see elk. So let's say that you have setup in a way in which the sunrise is going to be coming directly from the direction that you are looking, the East. This is going to make it difficult for you to see elk as you will be blinded by the bright sun shining directly into your face.

The second reason is that elk are impacted in a similar manner to humans by the bright light of the sun. When elk walk directly into the sun, it is more challenging for them to see every little detail that is out in front of them due to the bright light. The great thing is that you can use this to your benefit because if you setup with the sun at your back the elk will be forced to look into the sun and this can reduce the chances of you being spotted. So as a general rule of thumb setup with the sun to your back and be setup in the shade.

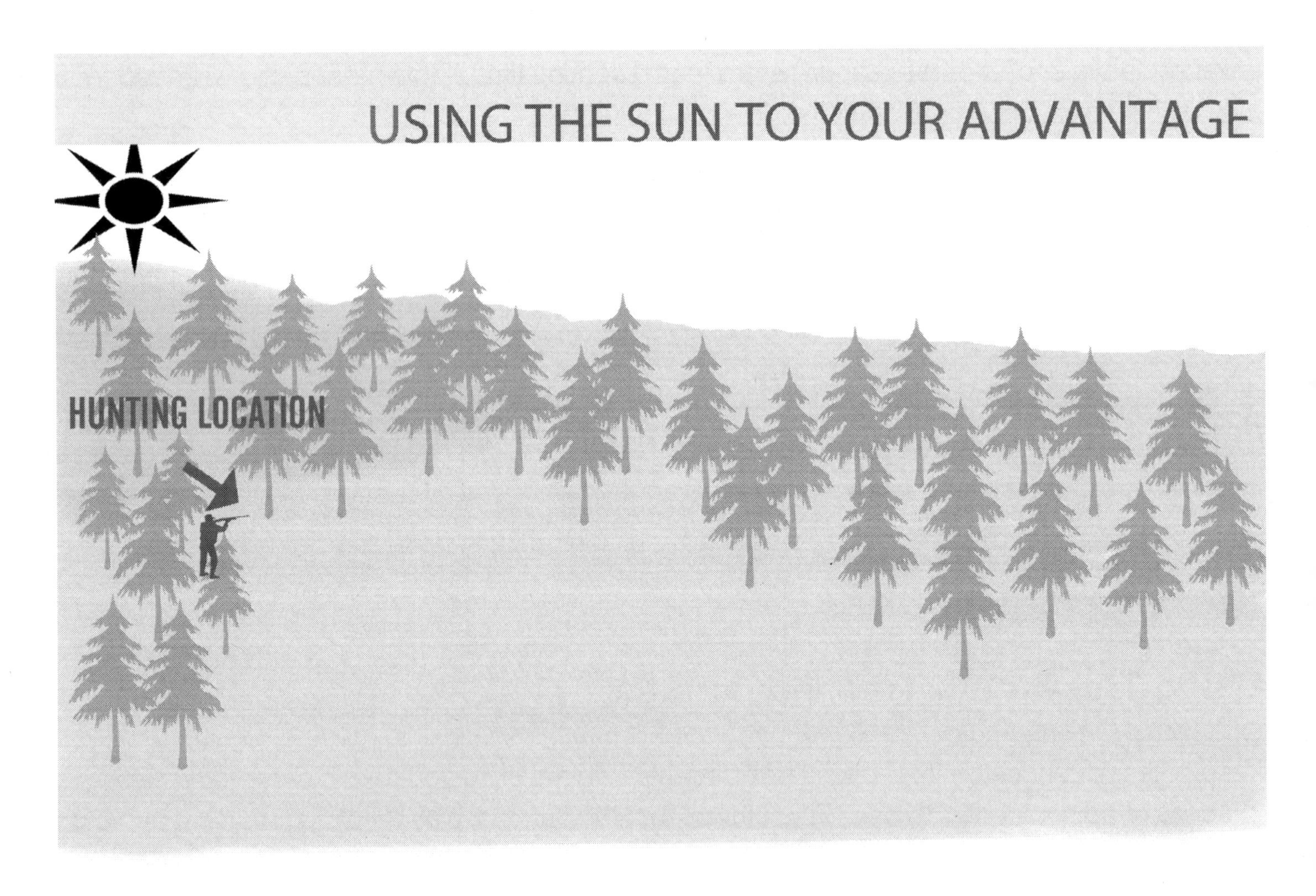

This above example shows how the sun can be of benefit to you as a elk hunter. You can see that the sun is to the left of the image which means the sun is at the hunters back. As the elk approaches, they will be looking in the direction that the sun is shining from and that can hinder their ability to see anything out in front of them.

In this example I want to show you what to try and avoid in regards to sun. You will now notice is the sun is on the right side of the image. This means that the hunter will be looking directly at the sun as the elk approaches. Looking in the direction of the sun can be blinding and make it challenging to see the approaching elk. When it is possible you want to try and setup with the sun at your back.

Now let's take a look at how wind impacts your hunting…

Step 14: Wind Impact

Using Wind to Your Advantage

In addition to using the sun as an advantage to your elk hunting you should also consider how you can use wind to improve your hunting success. With proper knowledge of wind impact, you can use both the wind and sun to your advantage as you work to fill your elk tag.

Wind

Something that beginning elk hunters might not be are aware of is how the wind can impact elk behavior and your chances of being noticed by elk. The basic thing to know about wind when hunting elk is that wind sends odors in the direction that the wind is blowing. What this means is that any odors that are coming from the upwind side to where elk are located are likely to be noticed by the elk.

You must keep this in mind as you hunt because you will typically want to plan on approaching elk from the downwind side of them. When you approach elk from the downwind side, the wind will carry your sent away from elk so unless they see you or hear you while walking closer, your chances of scaring the elk off before you are able to shoot are going to be significantly decreased.

How to Know What Way the Wind is Coming From?

Sometimes the wind direction will be quite obvious if it is a strong wind. However, there are times when it is a little more challenging to figure out wind direction so here are a few ways you can tell what way the wind is blowing.

- Check your phone weather app for wind indicator; some GPS systems will have a wind indicator as well.
- Look at trees and see which way the leaves are blowing.
- Pull a handful of grass or dirt and hold it about chest high. Slowly let some out of your hands and see which way it blows.

- Buy a "wind checker" bottle. These are small bottles that are filled with a powder, and when you squeeze the bottle, they let a small puff of powder out in the air. You simply observe the direction the powder blows and that will indicate the wind direction. These are sold at many sporting goods stores and online if you search "wind checker bottle" and are just a few dollars.

UNDERSTANDING WIND

WIND DIRECTION >>>

Above is an example to help you visualize what I mean when I say that wind will carry scent to the elk. As you can see from the illustration, the wind is blowing from left to right so that means that elk will be able to smell things that are on the left side of the image because the wind is blowing the scent directly at the elk. In this case, the hunter is on the left, so it is likely that the elk will easily scent the hunter. Now that you understand how elk use wind to smell out in front of them

UNDERSTANDING WIND

In this example of wind direction, you can see that the wind is blowing from right to left on the image. This means that the elk is less likely to smell the hunter because now the hunter is on the downwind side of the elk. Any scent that the wind blows from the hunter is going to blow the scent away from the elk. This particular example is an ideal setup because the elk out in front of the hunter is extremely unlikely to scent the hunter. However, you still want to be careful of not being seen or heard by the elk.

UNDERSTANDING WIND

WIND DIRECTION >>>

In this final example of wind direction for elk hunting I will show you what to do when you find yourself on the upwind side of a elk. As this image shows, the wind is blowing from the hunter directly at the elk so there is a chance the elk will smell the hunter. So if you find yourself in this situation, you will want to try and work yourself to the downwind side of the elk to get a closer shot at the elk and reduce your chances of being scented by the elk.

In order to accomplish not being scented in this situation, it would be recommended to walk to the backside of the hill. Then move down the hill on the backside where you will not be seen by the elk. After you make it all of the way down the backside of the hill you can then walk back to the side of the hill where the elk is and work to find a good shooting spot. As you will now be on the downwind side of the elk the chances of you being scented are greatly decreased.

This is a very basic example of using wind to your advantage. However, this concept can be utilized in so many different ways. Really, the trick is to try and always be on the downwind side of where the elk are. For example, if you have patterned elk over several days and you know that they are following a certain trail each day you should decide what side of the trail to setup on based on the wind. You will want to setup on the side of the trail where the wind is blowing in your face rather than at your back. With the wind blowing in your face the chances of the elk smelling you as they walk down the trail is very low.

Scent Cover-Ups

Now that we have discussed how elk can smell well and that you need to use the wind to your advantage we should also discuss scent cover-ups. There will be times when you are elk hunting that you find yourself in not an ideal spot and your scent may be blowing towards nearby elk. To be prepared for these times you can use some elk cover-up scents. There are several manufacturers that sell synthetic and even real elk scent. If you put some of this on your clothing, it can actually help attract elk or at least help cover up the human scent on you. It is not a bad idea to have some of this to reduce the chances of scaring off elk.

Now let's discuss how to effectively be concealed to fool elk…

Step 15: Concealment

Staying Hidden from Elk is Critical for Success

Elk, especially the older and more experienced elk, are wary and will always be on the lookout for anything that seems out of the ordinary. You must keep this in mind as you determine where you are going to sit and wait for elk.

Ways to Stay Hidden:

- Hunting blind
- Natural covering
- Deer/tree stands
- Stay out of direct line of sight
- Avoid body silhouette
- Camouflage & face paint
- Ghillie suit
- Smell

Hunting Blind

A simple yet effective way to stay concealed from the sight of elk is by using a ground blind. Ground blinds are easily transportable which make them a great option if you want to try hunting several different places. Some people like to move locations if they have been calling for an hour or so without any response from elk. These blinds are like little tents with a zip-open door and windows for shooting. When hunting from a ground blind, you will want to bring some type of chair with to sit on because sitting on the ground for any length of time will not be comfortable.

One of the biggest benefits of ground blinds is that you can place them in high traffic elk areas that do not have much for other natural covering around. For example, if there is an open field without much for trees or shrubs the blind can be a good option. Simply try and find a spot that is relatively close to some trails that you have found frequented by elk that lead out into the field.

There are a few other benefits to ground blinds which include the fact that it will keep you out of the elements and comfortable. Like I mentioned these are like little tents so when it is windy, raining, snowing or cold outside these blinds will help you stay somewhat protected from the elements and much more comfortable during your hunt. The last benefit to mention about ground blinds is their low cost. You can find them on sale at hunting stores for around $40. Of course, you can buy more expensive ones, but for something to get you started an entry-level blind should do the trick.

Natural Concealment

Utilizing your surroundings to keep you out of the sight of elk can be another great way for concealment. Often times you will be hunting elk that are in an open field or prairie, and you will be sitting on the side of the field to stay concealed. The good thing about hunting fields is that these fields will often be lined with trees, tall grass, fence lines or even woods that you can use to keep hidden.

For example, the field might have a fence line on the side of the field and then some woods on the other side of the fence. This can be a great situation as you could sit below the trees with fence in front of you as you look out over the field. The fence in front of you should provide some additional cover, but you should still have good shooting lanes as elk walk in the fields.

With natural concealment, you can get very creative on what to use to keep yourself covered. Take for example when hunting a prairie that is very hilly, what you could do is lie down on the top of one of the hills and then look out over the rest of the field from this higher elevation.

The natural curvature of the hill can help keep you hidden as long as you stay towards the back portion of the crest of the hill, so the hill keeps you mostly concealed.

Deer/Tree Stands

The areas that elk live in are often areas that deer live in as well. In pretty much any place that has deer, there are likely to be some people that hunt deer. A great benefit of this is that deer hunters often use elevated deer stands for hunting, and those deer stands can work well for hunting elk. There are a variety of deer stands such as ladder stands which is pictured above, but people also use tripod stands which are stands that sit on a large tripod style base, so they do not need to be placed in a tree.

Regardless of the style of deer stands that are available to you on the land, you hunt these could all be useful for hunting elk. One clear benefit of using a deer stand is elevation that it provides you. Many deer stands are 8-15 feet up in the air, and by sitting in them, it will greatly increase the distance that you will be able to see elk. Another benefit of being high up in the air is that it takes you out of the direct line of sight of elk. This is because elk will be looking at ground level as they approach. However, due to the elevation, you will need to be aware that you remain within effective shooting range to the elk.

Of course, if you do use a tree stand you still need to be aware of concealment so that elk do not spot you. Also, and depending on the stand you have it might not provide much cover to hide your movement. So when you hunt out of a tree stand it is still important to not move very much because even though you are elevated in the air, it is still possible that the elk could see you particularly if you are moving around a lot.

Avoid Body Silhouette

Another tip to stay concealed from the sight of elk is to avoid a body silhouette. This goes along with having your back to the sun which I described earlier but what I am talking about is if you are standing or sitting in a location where there is nothing behind you then there is a much higher chance that a elk can see you compared to when you have something behind you to cover the outline of your body. Take the above picture for an example. It is pretty easy to see the person standing on the top of the image because they are standing on the highest elevation of the hill.

In contrast, the person standing below them would be much more difficult to see them as they would have ground behind them to help cover their silhouette. So the quick and simple tip about this is to always make sure that there is something behind you so you do not stick out like a sore thumb. You could sit in front of rocks, trees, bushes, fences or pretty much anything else that is at least as big as you are so there is something blocking out your body outline. When walking along hills try not to walk at the tallest peaks as again your silhouette can be seen like the above example. Instead, walk down the hillside about 20 yards lower than the peak elevation of the hills so that there is always ground behind you if a elk is looking at the hill from down below or from a hillside adjacent to the one you are on.

Now let's discuss how to use decoys to pull elk in close...

Step 16: Decoying

Use Decoys to Attract Elk

Decoys are a great tool for attracting elk. In many cases, you will be calling for elk which I will discuss later but it is important to note that using a decoy of some sort along with calling is can work well in bagging elk. This is because as a elk approaches the location where they hear the calling sounds coming they are looking to validate by seeing the elk that is making the sound.

Make sure that you place the decoys in a location that is highly visible to the approaching elk. You should try and place them on higher spots in the field such as ridges, mounds or clearings in the field where the decoy can be easily seen from any direction. This is critical as you want the elk to see the decoy as they come to the sound of the calls. Now let's take a look at a handful of options that you can use for elk decoys.

Examples of elk decoys:

- Inflatable Cow Decoys
- Silhouette Cow Decoys
- Collapsible Bull Elk Rack
- Place decoys out of direct line of sight

- Hunting without a decoy

Inflatable Cow Decoys

A bull elk during the rut is going to be actively seeking out a cow elk to mate with. So bringing a cow elk decoy with on your hunt can be one way to bring a bull elk into shooting distance. One option for cow decoys is an inflatable cow decoy. These decoys are designed to imitate the full body look of a cow elk. The benefit of an inflatable cow decoy is that that you can inflate them by blowing them up, like a balloon, with your mouth when you get to your hunting spot rather than having to carry a large and heavy decoy on a long walk. Once inflated these decoys stick into the ground with the included stakes and you are in business. A nearby bull elk that sees this cow decoy is likely to come in for a closer look. However, one downside to be aware of with inflatable decoys is during extremely windy days it might be tough to get the decoy to stay upright and in position as the wind can blow this lightweight decoy over.

Silhouette Cow Decoys

Another option for decoys is a silhouette cow decoy. Basically a silhouette decoy is a flat, two-dimensional decoy with the image of a cow elk printed on both sides. These silhouette decoys are often made out of corrugated plastic, cardboard and sometimes even out of wood. The easiest way to describe this type of a decoy is to think of a yard sign that is used for political elections but rather than being square they are much larger and cut into the shape of a elk. Then instead of wording printed on the sides, it has the image of a cow elk printed on both sides. Like inflatable cow decoys the silhouette decoy style is beneficial because they are significantly lighter to carry than a full body elk decoy.

There is one consideration that you must keep in mind with the silhouette decoy. This is the visibility of the decoy can be limited if the elk approaches the decoy head on. What I mean is if you can imagine looking at a yard sign while it is directly in front of you the wording is easy to read. However, if you stand to the side of the sign, you cannot read it because the sign is flat. This concept is the same for approaching elk. If they approach the decoy directly, it will be easy for them to see. However, if they approach the decoy from the side, it might be challenging to see. Some silhouette decoys have a string system with them where you can pull on an attached string which will then be sure to keep the decoy lined up with the approaching elk to ensure it is visible.

Collapsible Bull Elk Racks

In addition to using elk cow decoys as a way to attract bull elk, you can also use bull elk rack decoys. During the rut, bull elk are protective of their territory and are willing to challenge other bull elk to win their shot at breeding with a cow. One way to accomplish this is using a collapsible bull elk rack. These are essentially designed to mimic the head and rack of a bull elk; often times they are made of fabric over a curved plastic. The fabric has printing on it that looks like a bull elk rack, and they often have a handle so you can hold them upright as you hunt.

There are a few ways to use this style of decoy. One way is to prop up the decoy in some branches or brush so that the elk rack is visible from a distance. This way you can stand off to the side of the decoy, and when the bull elk comes to the decoy you can take your shot. Another way is to have a hunting partner hold the decoy off to the side of you as well. This way your hunting partner can make some movements while holding the decoy up which can create some added realism.

Finally, if you are hunting by yourself, you can simply hold the decoy and slowly walk towards the bull elk. However, with this technique you need to be extremely careful because you will want to be sure you can set the decoy down quickly and pull up your weapon for a shot well before you let the elk get close as they might charge after you.

Decoy Setup

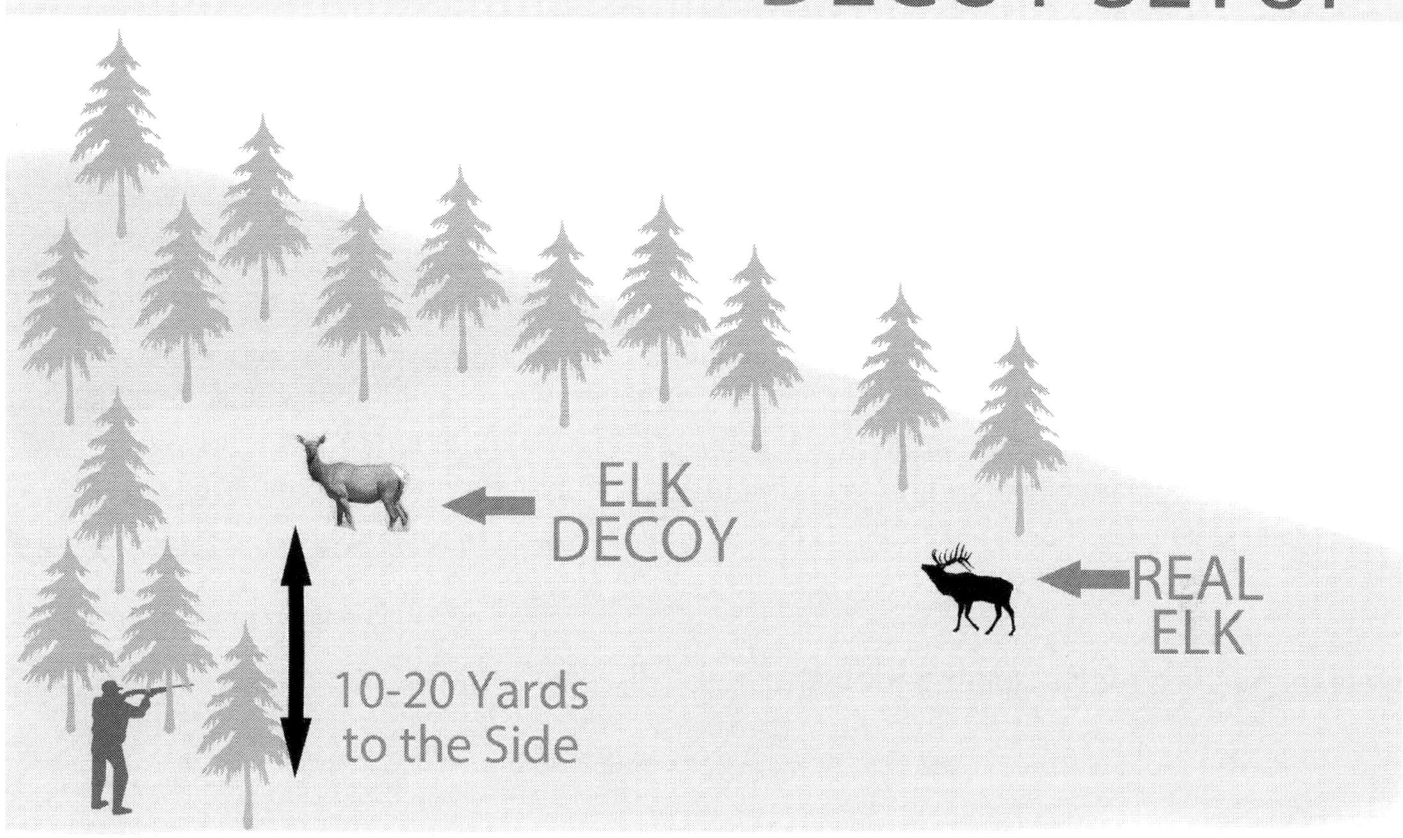

When you are setting up your decoy, it is important to keep the line of sight in mind to avoid being spotted. What I mean is it is not always the best to place the decoy directly in front of you. If you do this a elk that is approaching from directly in front of you would be looking right at you as they get closer to the decoy because you are behind it. Any movements or sounds you make could potentially catch the attention of the approaching elk and scare it off. To reduce the chances of being spotted set your decoy 10 – 20 yards to the left or right of where you will be hunting from. This way if a elk approaches its vision will be focused away from you, and you should be in great position to make a clean shot at the elk.

Hunting Without Decoys

Although decoys can be effective in bringing elk into range it is important to note that it is not necessary to use a decoy so if you do not have one or it is not in your budget yet to buy one you should not let that hinder you from elk hunting, people have plenty of success hunting elk without them. Without decoys, your calling techniques will typically be relied on more to entice elk to come to you through communication alone. One thing you may want to try without decoys is being set up in a location that is not visible from a long distance.

For example, when you are hunting with decoys being in a place where the elk can see the decoy from a long distance is a great idea as the elk will be able to visually see where the sounds are coming from. However, without a decoy being in a spot that is a little less visible can be effective as any elk in the area will need to come closer to check out what is going on so the elk will be a lot closer before they do not see another elk present in the area, by that time it will likely be too late.

Now let's take a look at calling for elk...

Step 17: Call Types and Sounds

Elk Calls to Grab Attention

Communicating with elk by calling them in can be a satisfying and unique experience. With some practice, you can become effective at drawing elk close which will greatly improve your success. In this section, I'll give you an overview of each type of call and how it could be beneficial to you. I will also provide you information on some of the basic call sounds that are used and provide you resources for learning how to call.

Types of Elk Calls

- Bugle Calls
- Mouth Calls

- Hand Calls
- Antler Raking
- Electronic Calls
- How to Learn Elk Calling
- Call Sounds & Timing

Bugle Calls

One of the most popular types of calls for elk hunting is the bugle call. Although there are a wide variety of these types of calls on the market the concept is very similar with all of them. The concept is you blow in the call on the narrow side opening, and the larger opening of the horn is where the sound emits. These calls are particularly effective in mimicking a bull elk that is in heat which means ready to reproduce thus notifying nearby cows of this. It also indicates to other bull elk to stay away. Cow elk in the area are likely to be interested in this call and will likely come to check it out. These calls are made of a few different types of material including birch bark as well as plastic or fiberglass.

Mouth Calls

Another option for calling elk is doing mouth calling. Now, this technique will likely a bit of practice, but the benefit is that you do not need to buy anything to do this. Essentially you will be placing a small semi-circle piece of plastic in your mouth to make sounds like a elk. Grunts and moans can efficiently be done with your mouth. One downside to mouth calling is that the range you can be heard from will typically be less than using a bugle call where the horn amplifies the sound further distances.

Mouth calling can be very good to use when you first get to your hunting spot. This is because the volume you have with mouth is less than horn calls, but that is actually good when elk are near. So after you learn mouth calling try this first in case there is a nearby elk since you do not want to blast out the loudest sound which can actually frighten the elk and cause them to leave the area. Mouth calls are also great because you free up your hands for shooting so when an elk is nearby you are always ready to tak your shot.

Antler Rattling

One alternative to calling for a elk is to do some antler rattling. If you have been lucky enough to have harvested a bull elk in previous years, you can actually use those real elk antlers to make rattling sounds. Bull elk will fight over cow elk by head-butting and knocking their antler racks together. So if you have the two antlers from a previously harvested elk, you can simply hit and rub them together with varying intervals to mimic the sounds that real elk would make if they were fighting. These fighting sounds can peak the interest of dominant nearby bull elk.

Antler Raking

In addition to antler rattling, you can also include antler raking into your elk hunting strategy. Bull elk often thrash and rake their antler racks as they travel through thick brush, saplings, and tall grass. This sound can instantly peak the attention of nearby bull elk, especially if the bull elk has a cow elk nearby. He will want to keep the intruder away from his cow so he will want to see where this sound is coming from.

One particularly way that antler raking can be effective is hunting with a partner. One of the hunting partners can thrash and rake weeds, grass, and trees just outside of sight of the bull elk. Then, while the bull elk is distracted by these sounds, the other hunter can sneak to a position where they can make a clear shot on the bull. To do the raking you can use antlers harvested from elk or antlers found after elk have shed them post winter. Additionally, items you can use for raking are canoe paddles or shoulder blade bones from elk or deer.

Electronic Calls

One final call type I want to mention is an electronic call. Basically an electronic call is a speaker system that you can place out in the field that plays real recorded elk sounds. Many models allow you to use a remote control to turn the unit on and off so you do not have to go out into the field to operate the speaker. Electronic elk calls range in cost from about $40 to $400 or more but can be worth the investment. However, you must note that some areas ban the use of electronic callers for elk. So before you purchase or use an electronic caller be sure that you check your regulations regarding their use.

The nice thing about electronic calls is that most models have a huge amount of sounds they can reproduce. This means that if you test one elk sound and with a push of a button and you can get a completely different elk sound to try and entice a nearby elk. Another advantage of electronic calls is that there is not the learning curve that there is with other call types. With an electronic call all you need to do is simply push the button on the remote, and you can turn on the call with extremely lifelike sound. This ease of use makes electronic calls a great option for beginning elk hunters.

Please note that even if they are legal to use in your area, there are some people frown upon the use of electronic calls because they feel that the time should be taken to learn how to call elk without the assistance of electronics. In addition, you may notice more personal satisfaction being able to call elk with a manually controlled call compared to an electronic call. You are welcome to make your own decision to use an electronic call, if legal in your area,but for those who are open to using them they can be an effective way to bag elk as you work your way to learning to use other call types.

How to Learn to Call for Elk

Because there are so many different call types to choose from and each call operates differently it is important to have some resources on how to learn to call. In fact, entire books have been written on elk calling and operating different call types. To learn more about how to use the call, I would recommend some looking at some of the following resources.

Resources to learn how to call for elk:

- Owner's manual may come with the call for some basic tips
- CDs sold at hunting stores
- YouTube videos (simply search for elk calling videos)
- Online hunting forums
- Fellow hunters

Call Sounds and Timing

When calling for elk, it is important to know that there is wide range of sounds that can bring elk to your hunting location. Additionally, each type of call sound has its own purpose to create a specific response from the nearby elk. For example, a cow in estrus can let nearby bulls know that the cow is calm and open to having a bull approach her.

Types of elk calls:

- **Calf In Distress**- The sounds of a calf elk in distress are very enticing for cow elk. Even if the calf is not from that particular cow, they will still be curious to come and check out what is going on. So if you are trying to bag a cow elk, the calf distress sound can be very effective.
- **Cow In Estrus**- One of the most commonly recognizable sounds made by a cow elk in heat. It is a cow elk call trying to get a nearby bull to make its final approach.

- **Cow Broadcast**- This is known as one of the locator type calls meaning it can be a great call to make to see if other elk are in the area. This is a longer drawn out call lasting about 8 to 10 seconds with the intent of broadcasting the sound long distances to get the initial interest of a nearby elk.
- **Cow Estrus Whine** - Using this type of call can be effective in getting the bulls to make a final approach to your decoy or hunting spot. This is a lower sound the cow makes and usually last only a few seconds.
- **Bull Grunt**- Grunts good to use when you have an aggressive bull in the area. There are a few different types of bull grunt variations with all trying to be a lower sound. Simply do a Youtube search for elk bull grunts, and you will hear many variations that you can try.
- **Cow & Bull Mix**–As you get more comfortable with calling another good call can be mixing a cow call along with a bull call. This can bring in other bulls curious to see about the possible mating sequence of this bull and cow pair.

I do want to point out that this is a list of some of your most common elk call sounds along with the basic purpose that each one serves in successful elk hunting. Please be aware that there is wide range of variations to each of these as well as many other calls that can be effective as you expand your elk hunting calling skills. As a beginning to intermediate elk hunter, I would recommend that you start with the basic call types as you work to get experience and success.

After you start mastering some of these calls, then it is great to add some additional sounds to your elk calling vocabulary. However, it is best not to complicate things as you get into the sport and risk becoming frustrated. There is a ton to learn with elk hunting so start to build your skills and expand from there. Think of it like riding a bike, when you first learn it is about the basics of balancing, starting and stopping. You do not start off riding wheelies and jumping curbs. Those are all fun things to add down the road, but you must first start with a good foundation before expanding into more advanced tactics.

Calling Frequency

Another consideration with calling elk is the calling frequency as you work elk into your hunting area. What I mean by calling frequency is how often you call for elk.You could elect to continually call for elk until you get one to come in or you may only call a few times in hopes of pulling in elk. What is the perfect amount of calling? Well, this is really where experience and trial and error comes into play. Some people call for elk every few minutes while other elk hunters call just a handful of times per hour.

People have had plenty of success with both methods, and it is really up to you to try out and see what works best for you and your area or even the specific elk you have near you. For example, if you have a very vocal elk responding to you with every call you make, then it might be good to keep calling back every few minutes. However, you may have times where the calls are more intermittent, and it can work to cycle your calling and give 10 -15 minutes or even longer in between calls. Again, there is really no perfect answer to the amount of calling because people have had success with all frequencies and each individual elk may react differently.

What If You Don't Get Any Response?

There will be times when you call for elk and do not get a response. Hopefully, you have used the tips about scouting your hunting area in advance to do your best to confirm that there are elk around. However, there will be times when the elk have moved out or are just not cooperating that day. It is essential to give each hunting spot a good amount of time calling to see if you get a response. There will be times that it takes longer for elk to react or come within range to be able to hear your calls so you must be patient. In fact, if there is a elk in the distance, it could take a day or more before they respond to the call or come in close enough to be able to shoot.

If possible, try and have 2-3 hunting spots scouted out and ready to hunt. It is going to take more time and effort to have a few spots lined up, but this will give you some great flexibility on the times you do get out hunting. If you setup at one of your hunting locations and call for a while without response then at least you have an option to pack up and head to the next location.

Also, note that if you have called for a elk all day and you finally get a response just before dark it is best to leave the area quietly and try the following morning. For example, if there are only a few minutes left of legal shooting time and the response you get from a elk is distant you should leave the area. Unless the elk is extremely close the chance of the elk getting in range before legal hunting time is done is unlikely. However, if you leave the area and try first thing in the morning, there is a good chance that the elk has come even closer making your morning hunt primed for success.

One final note is that elk sometimes do not respond if there are predators nearby. For example, if they have spotted a wolf or bear it is common for elk to stay quiet. It does not mean that they are not making it to your location, but it just means you have to have patience. As I mentioned earlier try several different calling intervals and see what works. Even if there is no response it is important to sit still for some time to see of a silent elk is on its way to you.

Now let's talk about still hunting...

Step 18: Still Hunting

Bring the Elk to You

One common way to hunt elk is the still method which is when a hunter sets up for hunting in one spot and calls to bring the elk within shooting distance. This can be an enjoyable and relaxing way to hunt elk because once you get your hunting spot, decoys setup (if you are using any)you simply sit back to call elk and enjoy the outdoors as you wait for elk to come.

Considerations for Still Hunting:

- Shooting distance
- Find a funnel
- Create your own trails
- Scanning for elk

Shooting distance

When you are trying to figure out your exact spot, you will sit for your still elk hunting you want to be aware of the shooting distance. This will depend on the type of weapon you will be using. For bow hunting ideally 15-25 yards is great but even up to 40 yards can be accomplished with experienced hunters using compound bows. For those using a shotgun, it can be up to 150 yards and much further with a high caliber rifle.

So as you plan out the spot you will be sitting be sure you think about where the elk are likely to come from. If you have scouted the area in advance, you might have actually seen where the elk frequently travel so be sure that you get within a short distance to that spot. Even if you have not seen elk during scouting, you should be able to identify where common trails are that lead out of the woods or walking paths in the field that you have identified with elk prints.

Take the image above as an example of this suggestion of trying to stay within 10-20 yards of the decoy. You can see that the decoy is placed about 20 yards away from the hunter, so that means that if any elk approaches the decoy and is in between the hunter and the decoy it will be well within bow range. Even if a elk approaches and is on the far side of the decoy the hunter should still be able to make an effective shot as it will still be a shot of less than 40 yards. If you have selected a shotgun or high power rifle then, of course, your ranges for a potential shot can be greatly increased.

Find a funnel

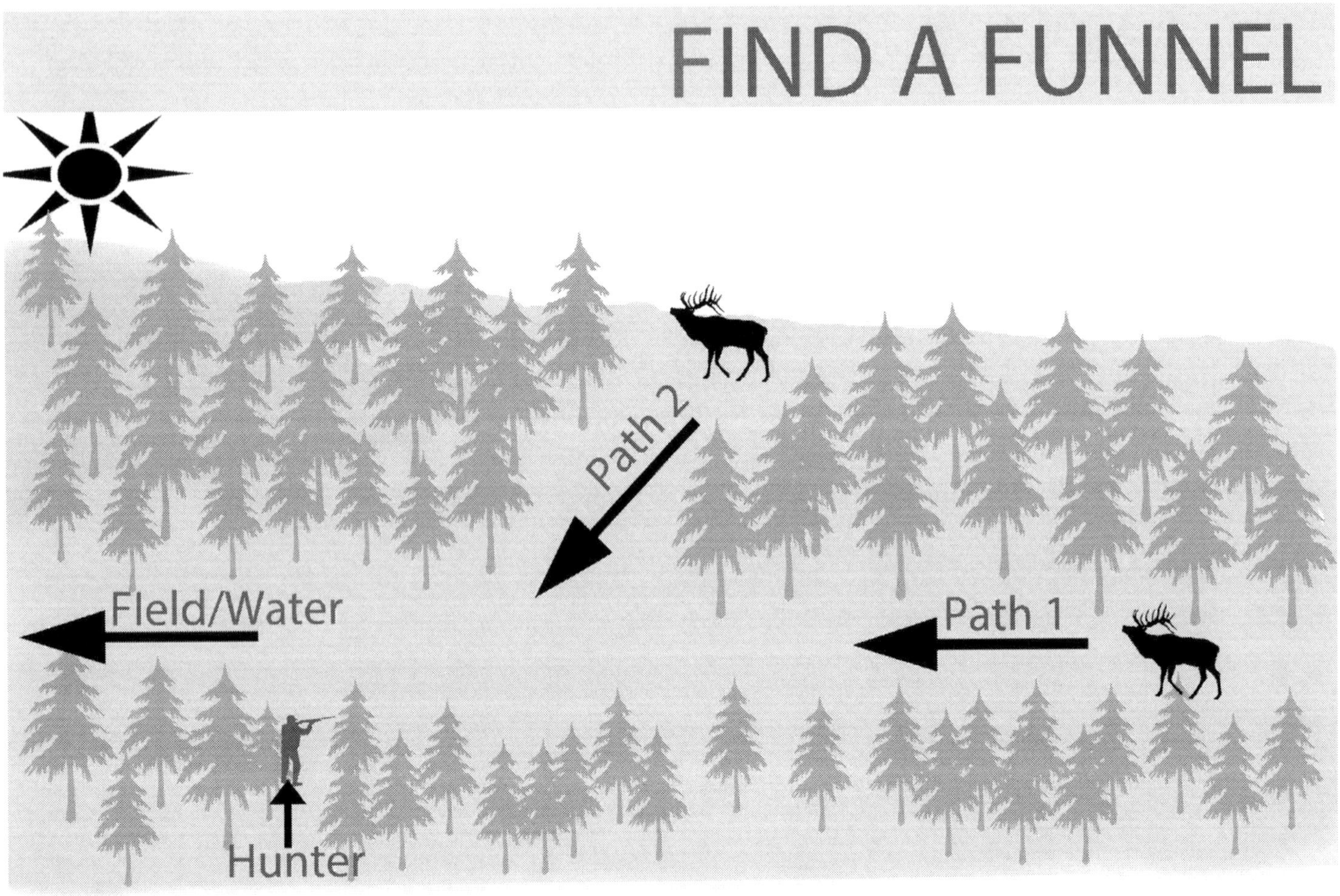

FIND A FUNNEL

This can go hand in hand with shooting distance, but it can also be effective to find a funnel to hunt near. This technique is more for use when you are hunting inside of a woods rather on open field. Essentially what you want to do is observe any natural trails in the woods that are frequented by elk and find spots where 2-3 trails funnel down to 1 trail. This could be a place where trails combine as they begin to make its way out into an open area or to water.

Those trails will act as natural funnels because the elk will be coming from various directions but ultimately to get to the field or open water there is only one clear path to walk through. Positioning yourself by paths like these can improve your chances of success because any elk walking that direction will only have one choice for a path to walk through so you can ambush them as they come down the path.

Create Your Own Trails

Depending on the area you are hunting and the trail system nearby it can sometimes be effective to make your own trails. For example, there may be trails running nearby throughout the woods, but in this case, none of them lead out into the field nearby where you plan to hunt. What you could do in this situation is clear a path or two from the trails in the woods and have those paths lead out into the field near where you are hunting.

You would want to do this a few weeks in advance of when you plan to hunt due to the amount of noise you will make and to allow the elk to get used to this new trail system. In order to accomplish the task, you could use a yard trimmer such as a weed wacker or even a chainsaw depending on how thick of brush you need to cut down in order to clear a path. This would need to be done on private land as public land typically cannot be altered.

Scanning for Elk

When still hunting for elk you will want to be continually scanning the area. A good strategy to implement is to scan from left to right and keep doing this at varying distances. For example, start by looking to the far left side of your hunting spot about 20 yards out and then scan to the right all around the same distance. Once you scan until you are looking all of the way to your right increase the distance you are looking, say to 40 yards, yards and then back to the left. Keep slowly increasing the distance you scan by 10-20 yards with each turn of your head. Once you reach the limit of your hunting area, then start the process back over. By focusing in on specific distances, it can help you look closer for elk in that area rather than trying to look at an area all at once.

Now let's identify tips for hunting elk with a buddy…

Step 19: The Buddy System

Use a Buddy to Improve Success

Hunting for elk can be a great way to enjoy the outdoors by yourself, but it can also be a fun way to spend some time with friends or family. Not only is it fun to share the experience but hunting with a partner can also help improve your success rate.

Benefits of hunting with a partner:

- Calling
- Two guns
- Extra set of eyes
- Be safe

Calling

One huge benefit to hunting with a buddy is calling for the elk. When you are hunting by yourself it will be up to you to do all of the calling for the elk so if you are using a horn call, hand calling or thrashing your hands will be tied up using the call rather than holding your weapon in preparation for the elk to get within shooting range. When you bring a buddy with you can share this responsibility and tag team elk.

For example, your buddy could start off doing all the calling, and this will allow you to focus completely on any approaching elk. After you have bagged a elk you can switch responsibilities and give your buddy the chance to shoot their elk. Sometimes a pair of elk will come in together, and the first person can shoot the first elk and the 2nd elk will stay around for a little bit allowing the person who was doing the calling an opportunity to shoot as well. Even if it does not work out where both hunters shoot a elk on one day, you could swap days until each hunter has had the chance to harvest a elk.

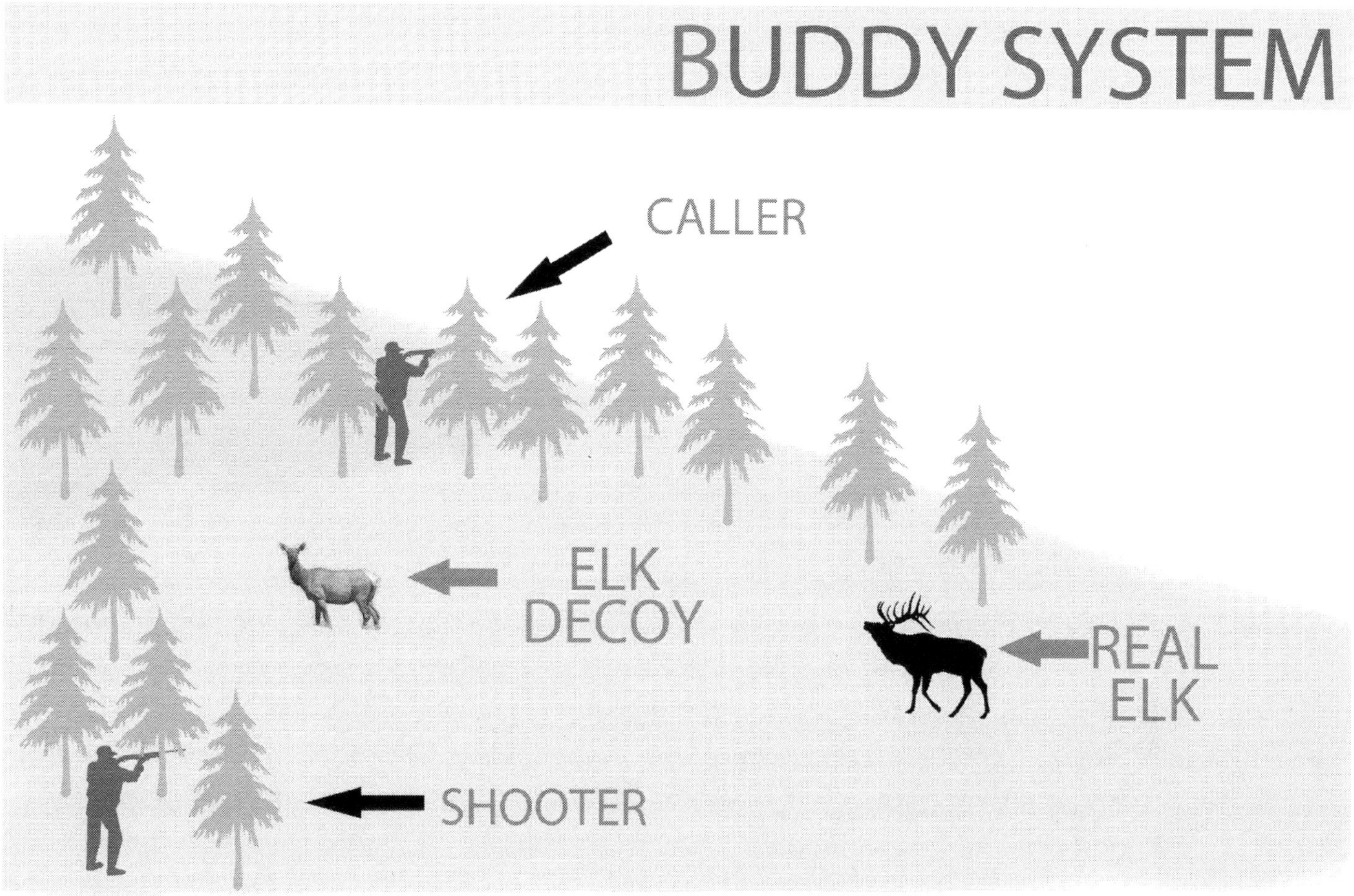

BUDDY SYSTEM

CALLER
ELK DECOY
REAL ELK
SHOOTER

Another benefit when hunting with a buddy is that you can hunt from different locations and have one of the hunters call for the elk while the other hunter is the shooter. This allows the sounds to be coming from a slightly different location than where the hunter is positioned. This way if the approaching elk is eyeing up the location where the sounds are coming from the hunter with the weapon will not be directly where the elk is looking. This can allow the shooter to get the weapon raised and ready to fire with a lesser chance of being spotted.

Two Guns

Another benefit of having your buddy with for your elk hunting trip is that you will now have two guns rather than one. Particularly if you are using electronic calls, you could both have guns ready to shoot. This could be useful if two elk approach at one time. The hunters could each pick a elk and at the same time shoot, so you hopefully bag both of the birds.

Additionally, with two guns one hunter misses their shot at the elk the other hunter could be prepared to follow up with a quick second shot at the elk before it runs out of shooting range. Of course, both hunters will need to have open elk tags for this technique.

Extra Set of Eyes

Elk can sometimes be challenging to spot, especially in areas covered with a lot of natural vegetation such as trees, brush, and tall grass. They can also challenge to pick out when you are trying to spot them from long distances. This makes it beneficial to have a buddy with as you can both be on the lookout for approaching elk as one of you may see a elk that the other hunting partner missed.

Try sitting next to each other or even back to back. This way you can each focus on covering a certain area while the other hunter looks at a completely different area. You can essentially double the area that you can scout by adding a buddy. However, it can also be useful to trade off areas that you are looking at. What I mean is that after 10 or 15 minutes if you do not see elk you could alternate the spots you are watching. This can be effective because after looking at one area for a long time you may miss something where switching things up and having a fresh pair of eyes look over the area could help spot the cunning elk.

Be Safe

Anytime you are using weapons it is very important to keep safety in mind. You never want to have a fun hunting situation turn into an unfortunate event and have someone get hurt. This aspect is increased when you are hunting with a buddy compared to hunting by yourself because you want to make sure that you never fire your weapon in the direction that your buddy is located.

It is important always to tell each other where you are going to be hunting from and plan out your hunting locations in advance and communicate this well with each other. Even when you have discussed hunting spots with your buddy, you should still be cautious when you are preparing to take a shot. Something may have happened that caused your partner to move from their planned hunting spot so be sure that you scan around the area that you are shooting at to ensure nobody is in that vicinity. If you are ever unsure if you are taking a safe shot, do not shoot. It is better to miss out on a shot at a elk over injuring a friend.

Now lets identify effective elk stalking techniques…

Step 20: Stalking Elk

Actively Walking to Find Elk can Produce Great Results

Stalking elk means that you walk through the woods, hills, and fields to actively find elk. Although this will require more physical exertion compared to the still method, with some practice and this can be effective way to bag your elk.

Critical Components to Elk Stalking:

- Plan your route
- Walk quietly
- Stop often and observe
- Always be ready to shoot

Plan Your Route

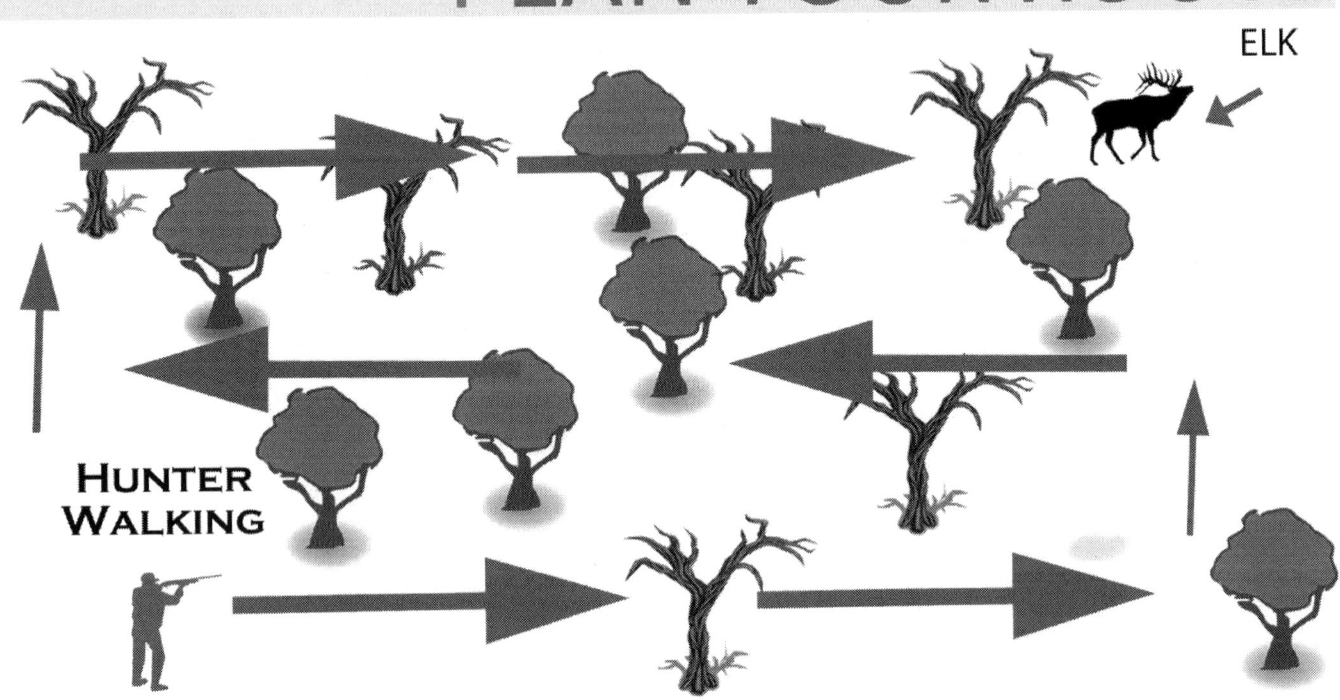

As you get ready to actively hunt for elk, it is important to plan your route. You should think about the area you are going to be hunting and try and strategize what the best way will be to cover all of the area in the most efficient manner. If it is a small woods you could walk down ½ of the woods and when you get to one end you turn around and walk back down the other ½ of the woods. For those times when you are hunting larger woods, you could try to zig-zag through the woods and eventually get from one side of the woods to the other. Just critically think about the best way will be to cover as much area as possible. You should also think about the high traffic areas for elk. Areas near young vegetation, berries, nuts and other food sources are places that you should be sure to check. Additionally, areas near water can be effective as the elk will eventually need to drink.

Walk Quietly

As you actively hunt for elk, it is best to try and walk as quietly as possible. You will want to lift your feet up completely off the ground with each step and take small calculated steps. As you set your foot down, let your heel make contact with the ground first and then gently allow the rest of your foot down. It is inevitable that you will make some noise as there will be branches and dry leaves that you cannot avoid stepping on but by consciously walking quietly you will greatly reduce the amount of noise you make.

Walking quietly helps you get closer to the elk before they take off. If you go crashing through the woods without any regard to how much noise you make it is likely that you will kick up elk that are too far away to shoot at or you will never see them at all as they will leave before you have a chance to see them. Being mindful of your noise should allow you to get to a reasonable shooting range before the birds are scared up, remember that hearing and sight are the elk best defense mechanisms so you must take every effort to approach quietly.

Stop Often and Observe

To ensure you have the best chances of seeing and hearing elk, you will want to stop every 5-10 steps and actively look around. When you are walking, it is hard to hear elk because of the amount of noise you make while walking but when you stop it should get much quieter. Listen closely for anything that may sound like a elk such as leaves crunching or branches breaking.

In addition to listening, you should also scan your surroundings carefully. Be particularly aware of any movement that you see and watch that area closely to see if it was a elk. Start by looking one direction, such as your far left, and then scan carefully from left to right. After you are looking all of the way to your right scan back to your left again. It is beneficial to do this a few times each time you stop to be sure you spot any elk in the area. If you think you saw something move, ensure you give it a few moments before you move because if it was a elk they will likely resume moving shortly and you should be able to spot them.

Mix In Some Calling

In addition to stopping every 5-10 steps to observe if there are any elk in the area, it can also work well to try calling for elk frequently. You might not call every 5-10 steps, but after walking for 5-10 minutes, you can try finding a spot to sit down and call for a few minutes. Pull out your call and try a few different call types. If you get a response within a few minutes then hold tight and see if you can get the elk to come close. If you do not get a response after a few minutes, then you can get up and continue walking.

Always be Ready to Shoot

When walking through the woods as well as open fields you should hold your gun in a manner that allows you to quickly get into shooting position. Hold the stock near the trigger in one hand and the other hand near the base of the barrel where you normally hold your gun when shooting. I can't stress enough how critical it is to the success of elk hunting to be able to shoot quickly if you happen to scare one up from a spot you were not suspecting one to be at.

After elk hunting for even a day, you will notice how fast they are and how fast they can run out of range. Even when you find a elk at a close distance, the shots are still challenging because of all of the trees, branches, and leaves that can be in the way. The quicker you can shoot, the higher your chances of hitting your elk.

Of course, you will want to pay attention to safety when you are walking with a loaded gun. Always be sure to keep the barrel pointed away from any other hunters and yourself. When you are traveling over logs and other difficult terrain you need to further increase your safety awareness in case you trip.

Now let's look at some effective shooting strategies when elk hunting...

Step 21: Deadly Shot Placement

Successfully Bag Your Elk

When you finally have a elk come into sight it is one of those moments that make your heart race. This moment can be brief, so you need to be ready to quickly take action to bag your elk. You must always be prepared because elk are leery animals and as soon as they notice anything out of order they will quickly run away and be out of effective shooting distance. Use these tips to make the most out of your shooting opportunities.

Shooting tips:

- Practice shooting before the hunting season
- Know your weapon
- Be patient
- Select a clear shooting lane
- Shot placement
- Improving shot accuracy
- Learn from missed shots

Practice Shooting Before the Hunting Season

If you have never been elk hunting or if you are having difficulty hitting elk then it might be a good idea to get in some target practice before you head out to the field. If you do not have your own land one of the easiest and most cost-effective ways to practice shooting is to visit a firing range.Chances are you live within a half hour of a firing range where you can pay a fee to practice shooting. This option is usually inexpensive as you can buy a time slot, usually in hour or half hour increments, for less than $20. This minimal investment could greatly improve your success on your next hunting trip.

However, it is not always necessary to go to a firing range. If you own your own land, you could certainly use that to practice. Or if the land that you are going to be doing your elk hunting on is available for target practice, you could use that as well. The one thing to keep in mind is if you do plan on target practicing on the same land that you will be hunting on I would recommend doing it many days or even weeks in advance. This is because it is likely the shooting may scare away elk so do this in advance to leave enough time for the elk to settle down and return to the area.

Know Your Weapon

Earlier in this book, I discussed several of the types of weapons that people hunt elk with including rifles, shotguns, and bows. After you have selected what weapon you are going to hunt with it is extremely important that you know your weapon and that you are aware of its capabilities. For example, if you have selected to hunt with a bow, you should be planning to take close range shots up to about 40 yards. This means that you need to get yourself into position for these close range shots as well as being able to estimate shooting distance visually.

Be Patient

I also encourage you to be patient when you are hunting for elk, particularly with shot selection. The temptation to shoot right away when you see a elk can be strong but you should hold back until you have a clear shot at the elk and that the shot is within the effective range of your weapon. Sometimes you may notice the elk head directly to the decoy and get quickly within shooting range. However, other times the elk will walk around for a while as they investigate what is going on. They are simply checking out the sounds and the elk that they see before heading directly at towards the decoy. Again, as tempting as it might be to shoot right away, it is critical to be patient and hold tight until you have a high percentage shot. If you shoot to early, you will end up wasting a lot of ammunition and scaring off many elk that you would have eventually had a better shot at.

The other part of being patient is knowing when to raise your gun or draw your bow. If you are able to see the elk coming from a long way away it might be possible to get the gun ready right away. However, if you are hunting with a bow it is pretty much impossible to hold the bow in a drawn position for a long period of time while you wait for the elk to get closer. What you will want to do, if possible, is wait for the elk to turn its back to you or at least to turn to the side before you draw your bow or raise your gun. This way the chances of the elk seeing you move will be greatly reduced.

Select a Clear Shooting Lane

Waiting for a clear shooting lane goes hand in hand with being patient. This is particularly the case for hunting in the woods compared to a field where there won't be many obstructions. You want to try to get into a position where you can see the elk and not have a lot of grass, trees, branches, rocks or anything blocking the way of your shot. This is easy to say but in reality, it is difficult, especially if you are hunting in a woods covered with tall vegetation. This is where some skill and practice come into play.

Many times you can only see part of the elk. The elk may just have its head sticking around the back side of a rock, or the elk might have half of its body covered by tall grass. Now is when you need to decide whether or not to take the shot. If you have a shot at the elk, regardless of how small of a portion of the elk it might be, you need to decide if this is going to be your best opportunity to shoot this elk.

If you think that this is your best chance, then go ahead and take the shot. However, if you feel that you may get a better shot if you wait then go ahead and wait. Shooting and missing is likely going to cause the elk to run away, and you may not get any other chances to shoot that elk. Also, a shot may scare off any other elk in the area as well so it is just important to make your best educated guess if you should wait. If you do miss try and not get to down on yourself as missed shots do happen. There is no guarantee you would have had a better shot opportunity had you waited so just trust you made the best judgment you could at the time.

Shot Placement

An accurately placed shot at the heart and lungs of a elk should provide a very quick and lethal kill. This is because the elk will die pretty much instantly from a well-placed heart and lung shot and it will make for a humane kill. Another benefit of heart and lung shots is that it will prevent most of the meat from being damaged because as long as the shot is accurate and the shot did not enter or exit through the shoulders.

Another benefit of a well placed shot in the heart and lungs is that it eliminates a chase to find the elk or a chance that you will never find it after it being wounded and running away. There is pretty much no way that when you make a clean shot at a elk through the heart and lungs that the elk is going to be able to run away.

However, heart and lung shots can sometimes be difficult depending on how the elk is positioned. If the elk is standing broadside to you the task of great shot placement will be much easier. However, if the elk is turned away, facing directly at you or away from you, it will be much more challenging. This means if you are a less experienced shooter your best bet might be to wait until you have a broadside shot rather than risking an attempt to shoot the elk in challenging body positions. Also, the further away the elk is, the harder it will be to hit the exact spot you want. One downside is that with a heart shot a elk could at last moment and you could hit the shoulders where a lot of the meat is contained damaging a large percent of the meat.

Improving Shot Accuracy

One of the best ways to drastically improve your shooting accuracy is to have a stable surface to rest against when you shoot. I discussed a shooting stick earlier and highly recommend it if you are hunting with a rifle or shotgun. This will help keep your gun from swaying back and forth which will create inaccurate shots. As I mentioned, there are times where you have to wait a while for the elk to get into a good shooting position so you may end up having to hold your gun up for a long period of time. It is surprising how difficult it is to hold your gun still with nothing to rest it on.

How to take better shots:

- Use a shooting stick
- Lean against the side of a tree
- Kneel down and rest your elbow on your knee
- Take a deep breath just before you shoot

All of the above methods are excellent ways to take more accurate shots with the preference of being the utilization of using a shooting stick which I previously discussed. However, if you do not own a shooting stick or it is just not practical for you to bring one with these other options could be effective for you. If you are hunting in the woods, you should not have much difficulty finding a nearby tree to lean against as you shoot. Kneeling is a good option if there is not another tree nearby that is convenient to lean against. Finally, to stabilize your shot you want to take a deep breath just before you shoot. Breathing causes the gun to move up and down. As you get into shooting position and are just about ready to take your shot, take a deep breath. Then aim and slowly let your breath out as you pull the trigger. You should find that this technique greatly improves the accuracy of your shots.

Learn From Missed Shots

Many elk hunters have missed at least one shot at a elk. It is important not to get down on yourself if you miss. Elk are leery and are not the easiest animal to shoot, so it is understandable when you miss shots at elk. Use missed shots as an opportunity to learn from your mistakes. Try to evaluate what you did well and what you could have done differently. Did you use something to brace yourself for an accurate shot? Did you allow the elk to get into a clear opening if possible? Did you shoot too soon? These are all questions to ask yourself in order to improve your shooting success.

Now let's look at some what to do after you shoot a elk…

Step 22: You Shot a Elk, What's Next?

After Shooting a Elk, It is Time to Retrieve You Game

After you shoot a elk, you will want to retrieve your game. Use these tips to collect your game successfully.

Tips after shooting:

- Wait a few minutes
- Pick out a marker where you shot the elk
- Walk slowly to the elk
- Check to make sure the elk is dead before you grab it
- Carrying your elk

Wait Before Tracking

Once you shoot a elk, it is normal to be excited and want head out and collect your harvest right away. However, you should wait about 30 minutes before going to find your elk. First, you want to make sure that the elk is dead so giving it a few minutes to stop moving can be a good idea. If you head out right away and the elk is still alive, it is possible that it will run off and go to a spot where you are unable to retrieve it. However, if you leave it sit for around 30 minutes, it will likely have run some distance but not too far, and it will be much easier to find. However, if you go after the elk right away and the elk is not wounded severely it is likely you will scare it up again, and it will take off running. This can increase the possibility that the elk gets away and you never find it.

The other reason to wait a few minutes before heading out is that there is a chance that there is another elk in the area that you can shoot. Sounds of a gun going off may not necessarily scare off all of the nearby elk so if they heard your calls or they are heading out to your decoy or were with the other elk but not yet in sight there is still a chance that more elk will come out of hiding. If you head out to soon you ruin any chance you would have had at bagging more than one elk at the moment. Of course this is only a consideration if the area you hunt allows you to shoot more than one elk or if you are hunting with a buddy who has a tag to fill as well.

It is also important to note that you should be careful to not misidentify your wounded elk with other elk in the area. For example, if you shot a cow elk, it is likely that her calves are still in the area. Or if you shot a bull elk, it is likely that there is a cow elk in the area that it was chasing. Given that most areas only allow you to shoot one elk you do not want to accidentally think you have scared up the same elk again and shoot it without being sure it is the same elk you already hit. If you mistakenly shoot a 2nd elk you would be in violation of that areas one elk regulation.

Pick out a Marker

As soon as you shoot a elk, you want to look for any markings near where the elk was shot. Sometimes when you shoot the elk, it will drop right in the spot it was shot making it easy to find. However, there are times when you shoot a elk that it may run for a bit before falling over dead. Particularly in those cases where the elk moved after being shot it is very important to pay attention to where you shot at the elk and take a mental note of the spot you took your shot as well as the last spot that you saw the elk as it ran away.

For example, pick out a tree, patch of grass or pile of dirt in the area that you can use as a location marker to walk to. This makes it much easier to find your elk. The interesting thing is that when you shoot at something a distance away, it is odd how hard it can be to find that spot when you start walking to it. The terrain can look different, and your depth perception can be thrown off. Also, your excitement of shooting a elk can sometimes make you forget exactly where the elk was shot. When you have a mental marker where you shot at the elk and the last known spot you saw it you can easily walk to those spots and then locate your elk. This way when you get to the spot you can begin looking for signs that you hit the elk such as hair or a blood trail. Once you find the blood trail, then you can track it much easier to its final resting spot.

Walk Slowly to the Elk

While you walk to the spot where you think the elk stopped, it is important to proceed slowly and with caution. Sometimes you may have just wounded the elk so you want to keep an eye on the ground and any brush or grass and look for movement and tracking signs such as blood and hair. On the chance, the elk is still alive and moving it may be necessary to shoot it again. Additionally, if you missed the elk or if it is just wounded there is a chance that the elk could charge at you. So out of your own personal safety ensure that you are on the lookout until you are 100% sure the elk is dead.

Check to Ensure the Elk is Dead Before You Grab It

Before you touch the elk, it is very important to ensure that the elk is dead. You will first want to stop several feet away and see if you can observe any movement with the elk. I recommend standing there with your gun ready in case you do happen to see movement you are in a position to take a quick shot if necessary. After observing the elk for a few moments without any movement then it is time to check if the elk is dead at a closer distance. An easy way to do this is by looking at its eyes. The strange thing is if the eyes are open that will usually mean the elk is dead and if they are closed it can mean that the elk is dead. The majority of the time it will be dead but if the elk show any movement at all you need to quickly finish off the elk.

To do this, take a step or two back and make an accurate shot at the head or neck. A head or neck shot at this close of range should kill the elk instantly. Be aware that if you do need to shoot the elk against a close range a shot to the body can do a fair amount of damage to the meat so to preserve as much meat as possible a head or neck shot will be in order. Of course, if you are planning on a full head mount for the elk, then you may want to take a shot further down the neck. Additionally, you need to be aware of safety with this situation because you do not want to shoot at something close to you and accidentally hit a rock or other hard object and have the bullet ricochet back at you.

Take Pictures

Now that you have determined that your elk is dead and you are about to begin the task of cleaning it you will likely want to first take some pictures. I mention this now because once you begin cleaning the elk, it is going not to look as good as it did just after you shot it. In addition, it is very nice to have pictures of the elk in the exact spot you shot it with some natural background compared to taking pictures of it when you have it back at your home. Certainly pictures taken with your cell phone can be sufficient, but you may also want to have a portable camera along for taking pictures as well.

Now it's time prepare and preserve the elk…

Step 23: Elk Cleaning, Preparation & Preservation

Success! You Shot a Elk, Now What?

Now that you have shot and retrieved your elk it is time to get it ready for eating as well as preserving your memories by keeping what you need to make a elk mount if you decide you want one. This part of the elk hunting process can actually be a big challenge. Elk are huge animals, so one person carrying them out of the woods will be quite difficult.

What to do with your elk after bagging it:

- Field Dressing the Elk
- Decide if Doing a Cape Mount or Antler Mount
- Quartering the Elk
- Transporting the Meat
- Disposing of Unused Parts
- Prepping Meat for Consumption
- Cooking Ideas

Field Dressing the Elk

You should try to clean the elk within 1 hour of shooting it to ensure that the meat is still fresh and does not have a chance to go bad before you get it into a cool area. If you are hunting in cold temperatures you can wait a little longer; however, if it is warm outside you should clean your elk as soon as possible after it was shot.

STEP 1: Lie the elk on its back

STEP 2: Stand by the hind legs of the elk. If there is another hunter with you have them hold the front legs apart. Otherwise, it can be handy to use rope to tie all 4 legs to nearby trees, so the legs are all spread apart. Use your knife to cut the throat of the elk about ½ way down its neck. Be sure to cut through the hide and all of the way through the esophagus.

STEP 3: Use your knife to cut through the hide and breastbone of the elk. This will be the part of the elk that is sticking up the tallest. Try and do this in the exact middle of the breastbone area. Do not cut any deeper than the bone as if you go further you can puncture internal organs which can spoil the meat.

STEP 4: After the breastbone is split, cut through the hide and neck the rest of the way up to where you cut the throat.

STEP 5: Now cut the skin the rest of the way down from the bottom of the breastbone area to the hindquarters. Do this by using one hand to hold the skin/hide as high up as possible away from the stomach area of the elk. Again, be very careful to not puncture the stomach or any of the organs by cutting too deep.

STEP 6: If this is a bull you will want to grab the male organs and cut around both sides of it, so it comes out with the rest of the organs.

STEP 7: Use your knife or bone saw to split the tailbone holding the legs together.

STEP 8: After the tailbone is split reach up and grab the esophagus from the neck area and pull it down towards the bottom of the elk. Along the way keep grabbing and pulling all of the rest of the organs. You should be able to pull pretty much all of the organs out all at the same time.

STEP 9: Once all organs are out of the elk, use your hands and knife to cut off any excess fat or tissue that is sticking to the rib cage hindquarters of the elk.

STEP 10: Lift the elk up from its front legs, if possible, to let any of the excess blood drain out of the body.

STEP 11: If you are doing this at home or back at your hunting camp and have access to buckets of water or a garden hose use them to rinse out the inside cavity of the elk.

Decide If You Are Doing A Cape Mount or Antler Mount

Now that you have your elk field dressed you will want to decide if you are going to do an antler mount, cape mount or none at all. If you shot a cow or calf elk, this will likely be an easy choice as not many people do cape mounts with them and no antlers to mount. However, if you shot a nice sized bull elk, many people want to preserve their trophy in one form or another. Doing an antler mount is the easiest to option as you simply need to cut off the antlers along with the top portion of the skull for mounting. This can typically be done with a bone saw. However, if you have access to a reciprocating saw the task will be much easier.

The prep work for a cape mount will take a bit of work. A cape mount means that you are mounting the entire head of the elk along with the antlers. These can be a great way to showcase your elk but do keep in mind the cost is quite a bit more due to the amount of labor required by a taxidermist. For cape mounts, you will need to keep as much as the hide possible around the neck of the elk. Typically, this means cutting a square section of the hide all of the way down to the front part of the front legs. It is a good idea to consult with your taxidermist in advance of your hunt to see what specific requirements that they have to prepare your trophy.

Quartering the Elk

Unless you harvest your elk near a road or if you are able to drive your vehicle close to your elk for getting it out of the field you will likely need to quarter out your elk. This means that you will cut the elk into 4 sections which will make transporting each section more feasible. First, you will want to start by cutting the elk in half width wise using your bone saw. This means you will cut the elk from the backbone down in between the 2nd and 3rd rib. When this is done you will have two sections of the elk. One section will have the front legs; the other section will have the back legs. Next, you will cut these two sections in half by cutting along the backbone on each section so what you are ultimately left with is 4 pieces with two pieces being the front legs and two pieces being the back legs.

Useful Equipment when Quartering a Elk:

- Hunting knife & sharpening sheath or stone
- Metal framed backpacks for carrying the quarters out
- Meat socks or cheesecloth for wrapping the meat
- Towels to wipe blood and debris off meat
- Rope to use to spread the legs apart when field dressing &
- Nylon rope ¼ inch in size for securing meat socks
- Bone saw for quartering the elk

These items are all good to bring with as a good assistance when quartering your elk. However, if you do have the ability to get your vehicle close enough to the elk and transport it for quartering at camp, then you could keep these items at camp. This will help keep your backpack lighter during the day hunts.

Transporting the Meat

With all 4 legs quartered out, it is time to get ready to get the meat packed out. The first thing you will want to do is protect the meat from dirt, dust, and bugs. One of the best ways to do this is to put each quarter inside of a meat sock or wrap in cheesecloth. A big reason that people complain of "gamey" tasting meat is due to improper care of the meat. If the meat is allowed to get dirty or if bugs get on it there certainly can be an undesired flavor of the meat. So by using meat socks to protect the meat, the flavor should be better preserved. In addition, you will want to ensure that the meat stays at cool temperatures. It is best to keep the meat at 40 degrees or cooler to ensure that the meat stays fresh and does not spoil.

Prepping Meat for Consumption

After you have the elk at your home, you will want to butcher the meat off the bones for eating. Before you start cutting the meat off try your best to trim as much fat off the animal as possible. It is ok to leave some of the smaller bits of fat but for the most part get what you can with a knife. You may also want to consider taking your elk to a butcher to handle this task for you. Sure there is some expense to having the butchering done by a professional but it will also save you a lot of time, and the butcher can cut and wrap your meat into certain cuts. For example, they can wrap your steaks and roasts separately making it easy to grab what you need out of the freezer when you are going to make a meal from elk.

Disposing of Unused Parts

After all of the cleaning has been done you will need to get rid of all of the unused parts. When you field dress your elk, it is typically ok to leave the gut pile of entrails in the field. However, out of curtesy you should pull the gut pile off to the side of main trails that other hunters may be using. The good news is that the guts are typically eaten up quickly by birds and predators in the area within a few days.

Disposing of the bones after removing the meat can be another story. Most city garbage companies will not allow you to put animal bones in the garbage. So before you do that be sure to check with your local garbage company. If it is not allowed a great thing to do is check with local butcher for disposal. They may have a disposal fee and allow you to dispose with them or they are likely to have suggestions of other local places you can get rid of the bones.

Consuming the Meat

Now that you have removed all of the meat from the elk or if you have had the elk processed at a butcher it is time to enjoy your well-earned elk. There are a ton of ways that you can enjoy elk meat. Really, most people will use elk in similar ways to how they use beef. Here are just a few examples:

How to Use Elk Meat in Meals:

- Hamburgers and meals that use hamburger
- Elk Steaks
- Elk Roasts
- Process into smoked sticks, summer sausage, and jerky
- Grilled Ribs

Final Words as You Start Elk Hunting

Congratulations! You have taken your first step in becoming a successful elk hunter.

Your Success is in Your Hands

If you have made it this far, it is clear that you are passionate about elk hunting and you want to shoot more elk. Remember that hunting is fun but also challenging. Regardless of the success, you have ensure you take time to enjoy the time you spend outdoors.

Just Get Started

Getting started with anything can be challenging at first. Think back to when you first started tying your shoes. At first, it was difficult, but after time it became second nature. This can be the same with elk hunting. The more you do it, the better you will get.

Make Progress Every Day

Using the steps learned in this book will help improve your elk hunting skills. I encourage you to make some type of progress each day of the season. Keep reading books, follow hunting blogs and watch YouTube videos. Six months from now you will be surprised how far you have made it by spending time learning more about elk hunting each day.

Made in the USA
San Bernardino, CA
16 April 2018